Just Aj!

simply stated

Simply Stated . . .

Enjoy your life and share it!

Aj

Aj D. Jemison

BOOKS
ISHAI BOOKS~EST.1998

published by Ishai Books, Inc.
4532 West Kennedy Blvd., Suite #435, Tampa, Florida 33609

Cover Design: Essex James
Cover Photography: Robert A. Sargent
Cover Concept: Ishai Books

JustAj! simply stated
Library of Congress Card Catalog Number:
2004104551
ISBN No.: 1-892096-71-4
The following poetry was written by Aj D. Jemison:
*The Stem, Oak Tree, Until-Big Mama, Inspiration, Jazz,
My Warm September, Where is Your Vision?* and *My Purpose*

PRINTED IN THE UNITED STATES OF AMERICA
FIRST ISHAI BOOKS: April 2004

Just Aj!
simply stated

Aj D. Jemison

These pages are dedicated to
the memory of my grandmother,
Angie Lee Lawson Henderson.
You instilled in me my passion
to care for and share with others.

Contents

While visiting my grandmother's house a few months after her death in 1986, I came upon a small, traveling makeup case on a shelf in the top of her closet. Never would I have imagined what it was protecting - the treasures of my past and answers to my life journey. I opened the latch not only to a makeup case, but to my own makeup, for neatly placed inside were funeral programs, certificates and acknowledgements of my ancestors.

Grandmother, the matriarch of our family, had collected at least three previous generations of obituaries, chronicling the lives of her family, my family. As I realized the precious gift that rested in this simple case, I was struck with the wonder of its wealth. Slowly removing and absorbing each piece of paper, I began to stack them on the floor in chronological order, then by family. The connection between each one was coming to life as names repeated themselves from one program to another. Here, on the floor of what once was Grandmother's bedroom was, I wanted to believe, a gift she had left for me. Unfortunately, the joy of the moment turned to sadness and disappointment shortly thereafter.

The sadness did not come in reflecting, remembering and reconnecting with an unfamiliar past of which I had not been introduced. Instead it came from the loss of that case. So soon after her passing, my mom wasn't prepared to part with any of Grandmother's things. I asked her to simple store the case for me until I could retrieve it when she was okay giving it to me. When I asked about it on my next visit to Tulsa, Mom had misplaced it and its contents. I have searched both houses in Tulsa, to no avail. It is unbearable to think that someone might have taken it for trash and discarded it... that could only be compared to the loss of another beloved family member – the recorded history of a family. I prayed that my past had not vanished, and fortunately found that a cousin in Malvern, Arkansas also kept funeral programs for years. It is my hope to visit Willie Clyde Lawson to copy and document some of the history he has in his possession.

The stories that thread together the lives that have expired in my family is my inspiration for this book. I remember viewing the teaching certificates, acknowledgement of school principals, and obituaries of musicians, carpenters and laborers that makeup the maternal side of me, the Lawson clan. These records answered the inner question that has replayed in my head over the years of why I loved school as a child, love to teach through storytelling and aspire to encourage the importance of an education. I am the future of those from my past that taught not only text book lessons, but more importantly life's lessons. I now feel obligated to share the stories I remember so vividly with others. It is my intent to inspire you to do the same. We all have a story to tell. I happen to have quite a few, so I will begin with this, my first published book entitled, *JustAj! simply stated*. Simply put, I ultimately wanted to record some stories of my life, a legacy of a girl from meager beginnings with Arkansas red clay dirt between her toes. From that little girl grew a mother, a professional woman and a motivational speaker.

As I tell my stories in the midst of my speeches and presentations, I am awed by the reaction and responses I receive. To have someone share that I brought them to tears because they could relate to my story is the genesis for my book. I simply seek to tell a story that will amuse, provide direction and a perspective of one single life, my life, which could mirror yours. This is my first revealing flight; join me in this journey.

Aj D. Jemison
Tampa, Florida, 2004

Foreward

Why I Keep It Simple (Purpose)

"You should take time to stop and smell the roses." Over the course of my life, I have heard so many people say this, but have often wondered where this saying came from and why they say it. After experiencing so many changes, heartbreak, joys and sorrows, I've learned these words speak to the importance of living each day to its fullest. It is through life's experiences that I've learned how important it is to keep it simple. I've learned how important it is to create and appreciate the most precious moments.

Just the other day, I saw a dad hoist his young son onto his shoulders so that he could see the world from the father's perspective. The look on the child's face captivated me as he squealed with sheer excitement. I could almost hear the thump as he wildly swung his dangling legs and crashed his sandals onto his dad's thick chest. It was incredible to witness his innocence and the absence of fear. Oh, to feel that again: secure in the knowledge that you can trust someone without question, concern or fear, confident that the stability of their love for you is unconditional.

We each have been provided with a special gift to see the world from our father's perspective... our Heavenly Father. For many of us baptized as children, we were unaware of the significance of that event. But as we grew and learned the importance of giving one's life to Christ, our eyes were opened to seeing the world through His eyes. It has been said with age comes wisdom, but the more profound reality is there is no fool like an old fool. The more we are exposed to worldly things, the more we lose our focus and sight of the gifts God has given us. We begin to trust in man or woman, rather that taking our trials and tribulations to the Rock where Jesus sits for our counsel and instructions.

When I consider all that I have been blessed with, it causes me to pause to say, Thank you, Jesus. For in Him I can depend to always be there. In Him I can count on when the burdens of life weigh me down. In Him I can turn to when I need someone in the midnight hour. With Him all things are possible. This I know, and this is why I continue to profess that I can do all things through Christ who strengthens me.

Instinctively a child trusts because it has no thought or reason to fear. Once we reach adulthood, I believe we all long to regain that feeling of security. At some time in our life, we realize that it, out ability to trust, faded as we grew older; washed away just like a sandcastle built on the shore. Can't you see the evening tide rolling in, time after time? The foundation of the castle slowly erodes until there is nothing left standing. Even though it was built with loving, attentive hands, over time the waters of the sea, even the ocean's gentle breeze melt the sandcastle away. Similarly, life's salty tears of disappointment, heartbreak and failures attack the foundation of security and fearlessness on which we once stood. Life's experiences, life's salty tears, slowly destroy our memory of when things were simple.

Forgetting to slow down and enjoy the beach, we often spend much of our lives wallowing in the midst of the complexities of life. We cry over the loss of one castle instead of seeing the great opportunities before us to sit down and rebuild other castles. You see, we have not forgotten how to rebuild, we simple forgot the reasons why we ought to rebuild.

I can honestly say that I have consistently found my memories of better days beneficial when the storms rage in my life. Within my memories are the many stories that bring me peace and give others hope. I keep it simple by going to the Lord in prayer. It is through our relationship that He demonstrates His love for me without judgement or conviction. I am thankful for that love, and the many gifts He has granted me, including the completion of this book that chronicles my journey thus far.

Through the rebuilding process, I've learned to create and appreciate all that life brings my way. I've even learned how to keep it simple. I am now at least pausing to smell some roses. Yes, a child finds security in its father's arms. I can honestly say that I have found an occasional sense of security in the arms of my "honey". But nothing compares to the incredible salvation found in the arms of my Heavenly Father. There I can rejoice, cry and shout. There I can be myself. There I can simply keep it simple.

Life Cycle One:

FAMILY MATTERS

Collection of Brown Angels (Family)

The greatest reward and benefit of living is the love of family. The collection of biologically similar individuals can bring more joy and sorrow to you than any other source. I'd have to admit that my family is the same, filled with its share of drama queens, and rolling stones, but never a more caring and supportive family will you find. They represent the angels in my life, as I watch them take flight, some faltering, others soaring, yet all in some stage of movement, never completely still.

Angels are messengers from God, and fortunately He has graced each member of my family with unique talents, skills and messages to share with others. From the clarinet, trumpet, piano and drums we played as children, to the decisions we made as adults, we use our tongues to speak, to sing and to curse. We use our ears to listen, to hear and to tune out. We use our arms to embrace, to lift up and to protect. We use our eyes to observe, to witness and to delve into the souls of others.

Remembering the words and advice of my grandmother to "love your family but don't neglect to love yourself," I finally moved away from home for the last time before my 30th birthday to get away from the demands of my family. Somehow I felt there was no room left for me to take care of me. If I had remained in Tulsa, I quite possibly would have lost myself, drowning in the continuing need to always be the one to help solve the problems of others, even if it meant causing some for me.

My greatest regret is that my decision to leave Oklahoma limited the opportunities for my children to grow up as I did. Leaving meant they missed experiencing the comfort and confidence I found in the love of my grandparents, cousins, aunts and uncles. I spent the next twenty years trying to find ways to over-compensate for the family I deprived my kids from having. Granted, it forced them to be more resilient, which may be a good thing considering the challenges they will face. I encourage them to stay in contact with both sides of their bloodline. For, like many 21st century African American families, our bloodstream embodies a fluid mixture representing the ingredients of our ancestry and heritage... a family hue ranging from a deep dark chocolate to a sweet creamy caramel.

There is one thing I can attest to about a family... in times of hardship and troubles, like an angel, the comfort of a family will never let you down. The selfish need for my own space caused my daughter and son to be much more dependent on me than they naturally should have been. Despite my late efforts to wean them from my support both physically and financially, their dependency, in my opinion, slowed their growth and ability to step out on their own at an early age. Another regret? Yes, to a small extent, but this is one that I can live with. My love for them has and continues to be unconditional.

My mom dubbed me her 'angel' when I was a little girl, so it wasn't surprising when I began to collect brown angels several years ago. It was my own way of replacing the angels I had left behind, my family and my friends. My assortment of angels has extended beyond statues, paintings, figurines and dolls. From my travels across the country, I have added an extension of families and friends. I consider them to be the most precious additions to my collection of brown angels.

Angels are the essence of consciousness, which causes me to be mindful of what is truly important in life. The angels residing in Arkansas and Oklahoma inspire me the most. They are the origin of my birth, having raised and supported me through whatever came my way. What a glorious collection of brown angels I have in my life. From the "other mothers" who cared for me and my children in each state we have resided, to the "play" sistas, brothas and cousins who befriended me over the years. Yes, angels are messengers, and the message that has replayed itself loud and clear from their lips to my heart is, "You are worthy, you are special, you are deserving of anything you desire". And now, family, I believe it!

Simply Stated:

So I ask you, who are your angels?   Have you recently acknowledged their existence and thanked them for their contribution to your life?   Take the time to share your life stories with a child or a young adult. They so desperately need to be inspired and motivated.   They are so afraid of the darkness in this world. Be their beacon of light. Share with them some of your challenges, trials and tribulations, including your triumphs and the rewards of your persistence. For, surely you have them, everyone does.   And as you remember the goodness in your life, as you search your mind to find the turning points and the journeys that took you from the valleys to the hilltops, remember this. There was always an angel watching, guiding and protecting you. You have survived despite the obstacles. It is your turn to transform into an angel messenger. The rewards await you, and trust me, they will be more valuable than gold.

Angels are inspirations that float through space, on a gentle breeze that lifts their wings, permitting them to soar.

"We must go back and reclaim our past so we can move forward;
So we can understand why and how we can be who we are today."

Sankofa

All the Days of My Life (Memories)

Someone recently asked me what I would do if I were told I only had one week left to live. To my own surprise, I had an immediate answer without having to give it much thought. Within the confines of only seven days I would take my daughter and son back to Oklahoma to spend my final hours with family...my mom, dad, siblings, nieces and nephews... to reflect on and create final memories.

Each room in that old house I grew up in on Cheyenne Avenue possesses its own history. In any given day, you might hear a variation of sounds permeating the walls. It can go from the soft snore of my dad behind the doors leading to the master bedroom, with its added locks still in place on the door to keep us out when we were kids; to the swishing of the washer and dryer vibrating on the back porch. The flush of the toilet in the wee hours of the morning signals mom's early visit to the bathroom, followed by running water in the kitchen and the smell of freshly brewed Folgers coffee in a fifth generation pot stained with nearly as many decades of use.

"I said, get up, lazybones! Don't let me have to call you again!" The tone of Mom's voice went from a plea to an order that we "get up" for the umpteenth time, as we tried to get that last wink of sleep. One-by-one everyone gathered in the dining room for breakfast. And like most Black families in our aged neighborhood, the heart of the day is centered around the dining room table.

Meals in our house typically begin with a breakfast consisting of dad's skillet potatoes and onions, perfectly crisp bacon and several slices of bread slightly over-toasted on the edges, still soft in the middle from the butter melted by the heat of the broiler in the oven. Everyone gets eggs only one of two ways, over-easy or scrambled. If you want them any other way, mom will tell you with a quickness, "you need to make them yourself." Occasionally there is a pot of Cream of Wheat or a plate of saucer-size pancakes. Yes, breakfast would definitely be on the list of memories I would want to leave this earth.

Lunch is a leftover thing, consisting of whatever you can find in the refrigerator or pantry. In the upper freezer of the refrigerator you can always find a gallon of Vanilla Braum's

Ice Cream. Dad loves when I come back home to visit because it is guaranteed that I will buy several gallons of flavored ice creams. Since mom doesn't normally permit him to have any, and of course I can't eat them all,   dad gets to feast long after I've left.

The   lower   half   of   the   refrigerator   is   always overflowing with enough leftovers to feed a little league baseball team. It's always self-service, so if you think that last pork chop from the night before is still going to be there the next afternoon, you are in for a rude awakening. Anything goes for food placed in the fridge unless you put your name on it, and it's not guaranteed to still be there later. The only way to ensure that no one will touch your favorite dish is to have everyone witness you do something to it, like swirl your finger around in it or lick it. That works every time.

A single doorway separates the kitchen from the dining room. A smaller table in the corner of the kitchen suffices for quick meals for mom, dad and the grandkids. Basically, the dining room is only used when family or company comes to eat. A crystal chandelier centrally positioned hanging over the formal dining table between two china cabinets, filled with the "good" dishes and silverware to impress company, is one of mom's prized possessions. The number of crystal teardrops doesn't come close to matching the number of tales told beneath that shimmering light fixture.

If I had to choose between breakfast and dinner for the most entertaining meal, it would be a toss up. I'd have to say the difference is that by dinner time all the events of that day are added to the conversation. It doesn't matter who starts talking right after the blessing of the food. By the end of chowing down, everyone has contributed to the happenings, jokes, exaggerations, lies and the laughter. We really get loud sitting around the table, mostly because you can't tell a good story without being animated. Since we have a family filled with drama kings and queens, you have to jock for your position to be heard. There could be as many as three stories going on all at once, yet somehow someone always manages to gain the attention of everyone else around the table with a story that grows, as every and anyone is permitted to add to it.

As much as we enjoy eating, at some point during the day you will find everyone making our way onto the front porch, where dad sneaks away to light up a forbidden cigarette. Mom, ignoring the fact that dad smells of recently extinguished cigarette smoke, is always the first to go back inside, saying she's either too hot or too cold, when actually it is just an excuse so she can go start dinner. There are only two or three rickety chairs with bent or broken legs to sit on; chances are you would be better off sitting on the front steps or standing. Storytelling resumes as the sun leans toward the afternoon. Casting a shadow and shade, a huge, fragrant magnolia tree looms over half the porch and house, visible from nearly two blocks away.   Considering the number of tornadoes in Oklahoma, if this overpowering tree ever fell it would take out the entire house, from the front porch to the back yard. It was this very tree that dad, in his healthier days, would climb to string lights to brighten the neighborhood during the holidays. This tree takes up most of the fenced-in front yard, producing the sweetest smelling blooms. Mom loves to clip the flowers and place them in dishes throughout the living room and den when guests come over. Kids love to swing and play on the huge tree limbs, while the men folk start talking sports.

To anyone passing by there is no doubt that a family lives and loves in this yard. You can just tell by witnessing my brother Robert riding on our niece's tricycle or the laughter as the kids do flips in the grass and fall on their bottom. Of course, then there is the baton twirling competition between me and my sister to see who can still "bring it". Even at my forty-plus years, I can still whip it, toss and twirl it fast and high. It has been one of the few physical talents that I can still attest to. "How you doing?" from someone on the porch, or a hand wave for neighbors driving by, shows our friendly nature. With the buzz of a lawnmower nearby or the vibration of the bass from a car full of teenagers cruising up the block, there is life on Cheyenne Avenue, and on our front porch.

Right before dinner is the best time of day to take a nap or watch a game or movie. For those wanting to catch a few Z's, you might find them sprawled either across a bed, a couch, or for the ultimate privacy on the floor under the dining room table. The rooms of this old house are somewhat typical, with a character and purpose that one might expect to find during the turn of the century. Over twenty years ago the den was converted from a bedroom my brothers shared as kids. Growing up in the 60s, the room was decorated to their taste, with its high ceilings and alternating walls once painted red and black with matching shag bedspreads and carpet. You would never imagine it would be transformed into a contemporary family room. With natural wood paneled walls, a rich, oversized floral sofa and dad's matching recliner, this is one of the few rooms where we let the outside world invade our lives.

The big screen television is left turned on most of the time, seldom turned off, just like the lights in practically every room in the house, to my dismay. Walking through the house into an unoccupied room with the lights turned on drives me crazy! I hate having lights on in a room that no one is occupying. Mom teases me how she can tell when I have last been home for a visit because her electric bill goes down at least twenty-five dollars. Now the television is another story. It only gets a maximum four hour reprieve per day. Rarely is there an argument over what channel to watch, since the house rule tends to be whoever gets there first gets to choose. Definitely the den is the "chill" room where you sit, or stand, where you can find a spot. And don't even think of talking while a movie is on unless EVERYONE else is talking or laughing. And phone conversations are not allowed in the den. Someone will loudly provide you with directions to another room.

Now I feel obligated to tell that although the house I grew up in is a very modest one, it was ours and under mom's attention we treat it like it's a castle. The living room at the front of the house is primarily "for company". The antique sofa and tables are a reflection of my mom's impeccable taste in nice things, just like the chandelier and the china cabinets. The mantle over the gas fireplace really adds to the mood of the room. This is the very fireplace that provides warmth and serves as temporary light during an Oklahoma ice storm blizzard. The upright piano in the corner and the stack of classical music played by my sister, Tori, represent the culture mom tries to instill in us. And my sister is not the only musician in the family. Tori shares her piano and singing talents with her daughter, Ciara. I was limited to playing the clarinet and violin, while Vic blew the trumpet, cornet and trombone. Robert's keen ear for music surpassed us all, as demonstrated by his ability to play every instrument in the house. The gift of voice was definitely only given to my dad, Robert, Tori and Ciara. The rest of us just need to stick to our wind and string instruments with their "pleasing" sounds. And poor mom, she was just plum out of luck all the way around, so we thank God for her ability to cook.

Speaking of food, the alarm clock to awaken those napping is actually the smell of soul food coming from skillets, pot and pans in the kitchen. For special occasions like birthdays and holidays, mom is known for cooking your favorite dishes and dessert. For my last 72 hours on this earth, it would have to be mom's macaroni and cheese, collard greens, black-eyed peas and chitlins. I love banana pudding the way my mom makes it because she leaves the bananas out of half of it, since I don't like them. And when she really wants you to feel extra special, she'll make two desserts. Fortunate for my older brother Vic, we share our love for German Chocolate Cake.

Dinner is pretty much a repeat of breakfast, beginning with the saying of grace to bless the food and a lot of talking with your mouth full. One of the most memorial blessings of

14

the table had to be Christmas 2002 following one of dad's lengthy illnesses. Dad started off in his typical soft-spoken tone, thanking the Lord for the blessings of the year and for bringing us all together for this holiday. But instead of getting right to the blessing of the food, he kept going on and on about what the Lord had done for each of us throughout the year, literally taking his time to describe each person's reason for being thankful. At first, we all just thought dad was having a moment, becoming overwhelmed with thanks because he had been so ill. But it began to become a bit much, with his occasional pause, then continuation of thanks. I can remember eventually opening one eye to peak and see if dad was getting emotional. To my surprise, I saw that I was the third of the nine of us that had opened an eye only to find both of dad's eyes wide open as he was praying and taking a bite of his food whenever he paused! He had been stringing us along and just wanted to see how long it would take us to open our eyes. Mom had opened hers first and had joined dad in eating from her plate, and finally someone started to snicker causing everyone else to open their eyes as the room filled with a roar of laughter and a final, AMEN.

Simply Stated:

Within the confines of my last 72 hours on this earth, I would give thanks for this day and all of the days that came before it in this house that I grew up in and the family I have had the privilege of being a part of. I would want each member of my family to continue these traditional meals and get-togethers, passing them on to the little ones, who are encouraged to participate. After all, this is what living is all about... family, and the stories of how we have lived and shared over a hot plate of food.

Forks in the Road (Decisions)

Being a single mom has been a path many young women have traveled, and although my journey may appear to have been a smooth one with clear directions, it was just as rigorous a trip for me as for most of the teen mothers that I know.

As I came upon one of my first forks in the road, I exited my youth on the verge of adulthood the summer following my graduation from high school. I surprised my entire family when I announced I had decided to give up a full 4-year tuition paid scholarship to a state university in Oklahoma, to get married to the boy I had dated since junior high. He was a year ahead of me and had already completed one year of college. So, in August 1975 I went away to Kansas to attend a college in the quaint town of MacPherson on a scholarship/work-study program to cover my educational expenses. We married on August 15th, one month to the date following my 18th birthday, on a small island in the center of a park in the midst of tall pussy willows. There were only thirteen people in attendance, representing my family, his basketball coach, teammates and the campus minister. Wearing the same ivory dress I wore a few months earlier to the Debutante Ball, I at least looked the part of a bride, even styling my matching lace Stetson hat with its matching ivory, short veil.

Taking his role as the Best Man quite seriously, my older brother asked what I was thinking as we cross the small bridge in the Kansas park that would take me from my childhood to womanhood. My response was, "I can't wait for this to be over so I can take off these tight, ugly shoes and put on some shorts and sandals". I had little understanding back then of the institution of marriage, and had given little thought to what my future would be. I was officially becoming an adult, giving up the chance to share a dorm room, never to experience study groups, pledge a sorority or witness a panty raid.

Immediately following the wedding we moved into the campus apartments for married students and began our routine, mundane schedule. For him it was class, basketball practice and hanging out with the fellows. For me it was class in the morning, work/study in the afternoon, cook dinner in the evening and studying at night. There were only two other Black girls on campus, one married to another basketball player and the other single and crazy. I didn't fit in with either, so I became a studious loner.

My life became a fast-paced roller coaster ride, and I was in the front seat with no one at the controls. I not only felt alone but it was magnified having left my loving family so soon after graduating high school. So what did I do next? I made a family.

Within my first two months of marriage, before mid-terms, I got pregnant. This was not an "oops", since I intentionally stopped taking birth control. When I think back on what the heck I must have been thinking at the time, the only thing that comes to mind is the fact that I had probably made a mistake by getting married so young. Yet, I was determined not to admit it, so I did what any other naïve, 18 year old girl who thought she was grown would do, I made matters worse. All I could think about was that I didn't want to be left alone, and that having a child would give me the permanent companionship that I so longed for. Desperation can result in really poor decisions, and I was a scared, desperate girl that wanted to have someone to love and someone to love me, at any cost. Knowing I had a child growing inside of me was an indescribable feeling, and I prayed for a girl.

That prayer was answered with yet another fork in the road. I gave birth to my daughter late the following spring, was separated and divorced before my twentieth birthday. I knew I hadn't found my home in this marriage. I knew what home felt like, so I went back home to Tulsa to find it again, only this time by living with my grandmother. I got a job so I could afford to raise my daughter alone, and I returned to school to better myself and overcome some of the poor decisions I had made so early in my young adult life. While I worked a full time job to help cover household expenses, Grandmother was a tremendous help by caring for my daughter, Franchiel, until she was old enough to start day care. Putting my daughter into day care was probably the one thing that Grandmother and I disagreed on. She desperately wanted to continue to take care of her until she entered kindergarten. I had to explain how important it was to me that Franchiel learn to play with other children. For all the love and wisdom Grandmother shared with me, I felt that spoiling her great-granddaughter would not be in Franchiel's best interest. Although Grandmother never spared the rod with any of her grandchildren, including me, she had mellowed in her old age. Of course, I never said that to her face.

As I encountered each of these forks in the road, I found a sharpened knife in unnecessary challenges and a spoon to catch me before I would fall. These came in the form of the many lessons I learned from my grandmother. My spirituality intensified under her watchful eye, as she shared with me the teaching of the bible. Grandmother was also very superstitious, even considered a bit prophetic. That was a trait she and I had in common, as she showed me how not to be afraid of my gut feelings or premonitions. She could tell through her dreams if someone was going to have a baby. The only problem was, she couldn't tell who! My cousin, Lynn, can attest to that. Thinking she had "taken care of that" and was done after her two daughters were born, she got her "oops", several years later.   As typical during dinner one night, Grandmother announced somebody in the family was going to have a baby. I knew it wasn't me, even though I had been trying for some time. Lynn was adamant it couldn't possibly be her, but Grandmother just smiled and said, "We'll see". And four months later Lynn delivered her son, Carl Jr, affectionately nicknamed "Papa". Before there were over-the-counter pregnancy tests and remedies, there was my Grandmother. Her hands may have had arthritis, but they could still sooth sore muscles, a headache or a broken heart. Her medicine chest had the basics (castor oil, Vick's Vapor

Rub, epson salt, a rectal thermometer, etc.), but she also used unorthodox methods of healing. Like how to test for mumps by biting into a dill pickle (ouch!).

Working as a domestic for many years, Grandmother not only cleaned after rich folk, she, like many others in her generation, raised their children. I joined her many times as a child on her workdays. When she couldn't get someone to drop us off, we'd take the bus ride to the South Tulsa home of a doctor's family. My tasks were always pretty simple. I would do the vacuuming and sweep, take out the trash, dust the furniture, help make the beds and bring in the laundry from the dryer. Grandmother did the ironing, cleaned the kitchen, cooked and ran errands. Every year the family would give her a Christmas bonus, a turkey and a bag of groceries. I still can't say how I feel about all of that except to say that I knew my grandmother was proud of the quality of work she did, and for that I was proud of her.

Now when it comes to cooking, well, that is another subject all together. Simply put, I couldn't boil a pot of water! Seriously, I remember trying to boil some eggs and forgot the water was on the stove. Next thing I knew, smoke filled the kitchen from the scorched pot I left unattended for over an hour. But I did learn how to make fried, hot water bread to go with collard green. To clean the house meant moving every piece of furniture at least once a month. And although I hated cooking, she did show me how to shuck a paper bag full of string beans on the front porch. Those four years that we lived together were invaluable to my growth as a mother and an adult. I was her work in progress and a student of life. I like to think she taught me well.

Simply Stated:

     The wisdom of a grandparent is colorless and ageless. It represents struggles, especially for those born before the 50s. What they endured so that we wouldn't have to is a testament to their love for generations to come. As you consider what role you will play in the lives of your grandchildren, take the time to reflect and remember what our grandparents provided us. They came to the fork in the road and chose a path. And even if they took the wrong road, there is now a road map that should keep us on a course less rocky than the one they traveled. They placed a sign at their forks in the road so that we would not find ourselves facing a dead end. The love in a grandmother's heart is like a boomerang; it will return over and over again, always hitting its mark with precision and accuracy.

THE STEM

I bet you never paid attention to the importance of a stem
Take a moment to ponder its significance as a flower's limb

Have you ever wondered how it manages to hold up a flower
With a long, lean appearance, its strength surpasses an hour

Look how it reaches straight upward as if to reach the sky
Yet it's the flower that attracts and catches an observers' eye

Have you ever stopped to admire the support of that bloom
The stem allows it to captivate an audience or a room

The flower wouldn't survive without the nourishment that flows
within
Yet, few pause to snip the tip of the nurturing vessel called the stem

It drinks to take in nutrients like tomorrow will never come
A thirst that's everlasting causes it to stand tall and handsome

Yes, the stem holds the secret to the beauty of the plant
It has a "can-do" attitude and never utters the word "can't"

It knows its purpose in life is to stand tall, firm and achieve
A foundation of God's beauty, in its own strength it must believe

So the next time you stop to smell a rose think of this before you pass
It is the stem that holds it up, and compared to the rose the stem will
last.

"Children are petals of a flower in bloom"

Aj D. Jemison

Birthing Angels (Parenting)

I wouldn't trade in being a mother for any material treasure known to man. There is nothing that can compare to the incredible exhilaration of this experience. However, the realization of this reality is a rude awakening.

No one tells you about the episode of childbirth where your oversized body squirms on a gurney no bigger than a twin-size bed covered only by a thin sheet, as you lay freezing trying unsuccessfully to find some semblance of comfort. At age nineteen, I reluctantly gave in to my private parts being shaved by a nurse-aide, and the insertion of an enema, which was already working. I couldn't imagine what could possibly follow. Then my water broke.

Women hold onto these fine details like the ending to a great mystery novel. How in the heck could I have known at nineteen, married less than a year, that there would be more to having a baby? I bought into the abridged version (some pain, a

Aj D. Jemison

few good pushes, the slap on the rear, and hearing the baby's first cry)… what a ridiculous understatement.

One of my favorite books, *The Prophet* by Kahlil Gibran, includes a poem on the subject of Children, in which I have found the ultimate reasoning and explanation for my purpose as a parent. In his poem he writes,

Your children are not your children. They are the sons and daughters of Life's longing for itself. They come through you but not from you. You are the bows from which your children as living arrows are sent forth.

Reflecting on the birth of my firstborn and how from the moment her small body left mine, I am reminded how I spoke to her as we met for the very first time. She was someone I had only known spiritually for the previous nine months. One would think that once you have given birth to one child, all others would be easy. Well let me just start by saying that I live by the phrase, "two and through", for I will not, thankfully, revisit this experience in my lifetime. As the rapid cries to, "Get down on your knees! Don't talk! Get me some ice chips! WHERE are you going?" oozed from my lips, I shouted orders all in one single breath to the one person responsible for my condition… Greg!

Childbirth for the second time involved hours of pacing the corridors of Hillcrest Hospital's birthing center where I checked in the evening before to give birth. It could only be compared to walking the Green Mile. The labor pains had stopped some four hours before, yet I refused to leave the hospital this time, despite being told it was a false alarm for a second time. I threatened to take up residency (and not as a doctor) if they did not break my water to induce labor so I could deliver this baby.

Yes, I refused to return home, since in any baseball game with three strikes, you're out and I had already been here twice in the past two weeks. I learned that rule of the game from Greg, after three year of sitting in the stands cheering for the minor league New York Yankees and Texas Rangers teams for whom he had played and coached. I was adamant that the doctor simply needed to break my water and we could get out of this ninth inning stretch with a grand slam homerun. This game was not going into overtime... not today.

The greatest gift one can give another is that of breath and the blood of life. I have experienced this joy and privilege, twice, first with the birth of my daughter, Franchiel, and seven years later with the conclusion of my childbearing days with the birth of my son, Houston. On the day each was born, I realized I was merely a vessel through which they had traveled.

I saw Franchiel as her own person even from infancy, her personality already established, astute, aware and cautious, suspicious of others yet wanting so desperately to trust. She has a searching soul, not unlike my own, as she travels a journey that I long to share with her. I visualize for her a future she can neither see nor fathom. As a mother, through loving eyes I can see the glow that exudes from her. Despite the window shade of insecurity she now uses to try to protect her sensitive self from the view of other, the day will surely come when her light will seep through, fully exposing her talents, abilities and inspiration to the world. Today is just a cloudy day. Soon she will realize that although she may feel fame is eluding her and asks 'why', in reality she hasn't been looking inside herself where it has resided all along. This Nubian princess will soon take her seat on a thrown, a deserved reward for the years of hard times for one so young, on her trek up the road less traveled.

My son's aura as he entered this world on the first day of August 1983 was a cool hue of blue. Born under the sign of the Lion, this Leo's roar remained a purr until he reached his manhood at the age of eighteen. Comfortable most of his youth in the shadows and the shade of the overgrown oak tree of a assertive older sister and self-reliant mother, Houston is observant, attentive and quiet, as his kingdom forms around him. There is no doubt that when he feels prepared and equipped, he will take over and rule his kingdom. In his own time and space he is expanding his territory, surveying the land

and charting a path. As a lion cub, he took on several leadership roles. A force to be reckoned with and a deep voice determined to be heard, his roar is as loud as his heart is big. A sensitive, gentle spirit resides in the soul of this strong Black man... my son.

As a parent, it is very difficult to simply be the archer's bow, willingly releasing our children as living arrows sent into the future which we can never travel. Some archers aim their bows toward the sky, only to have them rise swiftly yet fall just as quickly toward immense depths of disappointments. Others aim too low, wanting to ensure an easy success and direct journey for them, instead expediting their lack of drive and direction. The true test of a good marksman is having the strength to aim them straight ahead, knowing they will encounter challenges, hardships and even heartbreak. Allowing our children to experience these three risks will build their character, enabling and preparing them for the high winds that will surely come to lift them to greater heights of accomplishment beyond their own expectations.

To "reap what you sow" insinuates that you much work for your harvest. A gardener understands the importance of tending to the ground before planting the seed then watering and weeding the garden to ensure its growth. The gardener knows that providing tender, loving and nurturing care hopefully will guarantee a full bloom and profitable harvest. Then, we wise ones realize there are no guarantees. A thunderstorm of rain and hail can destroy in minutes what took years to grow. Yet, if that seed is carefully planted deep into the soil permitting the roots to expand and take hold, the plant or fruit will recover and continue to grow. The warmth of the sun will be its beacon, as the seedling extends upward, seeking and striving to survive.

Simply Stated:

We, as parents, are the only rays of hope and
nourishment that our children have. We had the benefit of
having parents who instilled in us what is and will be required
to survive, and it is that very resilience that we must inject deep
into the blood vessels of our children to ensure their growth
and endurance through their storms of life. We must take on
the full charge of the gardener, providing the nutrients of
encouragement, fortitude and reassurance our babies need. It is
our obligation to be held accountable for the outcome of their
lives. We must stop planting them on top of the ground to be
trampled on by the troubles of this world we created and left
for them to repair, recover from and recoup. How dare we
expect less of them than our parents did of us? Our parents had
a right to believe the children they bore would have a better
life.

We have the ability to live longer, better and more
productive than the elders that came before us who got us this
far. How dare we sit back and deprive our babies of a future
filled with spring showers, summer breezes, autumn transitions
and winter's splendor. The seasons should be theirs to
experience, appreciate and enjoy. It will take more than
speaking the words "I love you" to get them through as they

encounter the heavy downpours of discriminating hail storms, critical floodwaters and the unexpected lightening strikes of heartache. It will take committed action on our part to ensure that our children will develop, evolve and flourish into mature adults, prepared and capable of eventually reaching their peak to take in the spectacular view of a world and life worth living.

Invest in the future by making daily deposits into the life of a child today.

"Dedication to My Sunshine

I give you my past

from whence I came

I give you the present

of which I share with you

I give you the future

with its pleasures and pain

I give you my love.

"Laugh long, laugh hard, laugh lovingly"

Aj D. Jemison

Sense of Humor (Appreciation)

Every family has a comedian, whether it's Uncle Dail, Cousin Lynn or June Bug. My grandfather, Big Dad, took that honor with a great sense of pride to match his sense of humor, as he was dubbed the prankster of the family. Even at his funeral, the minister in our hometown of Malvern, Arkansas had stories to tell about how Big Dad used to play practical (and sometimes not so practical) jokes on him and other kids in their neighborhood.

My grandparents relocated to Tulsa, Oklahoma in the late 50s from the backwoods of Princeton, Arkansas. Claude Henderson married Angie Lee Lawson on March 15, 1930, their union creating another branch to this family tree from which I've sprouted. They managed to maintain and transplant their "country" way of living from rural fields to the big city, determined to continue to live off the land, remaining humble in the environment they created. From the outside looking in, you might see them as a Black family trying to survive poverty, but you should clean your glasses and take a much closer look. Their reality is that they were taught how to be resourceful, resulting in a house filled with gadgets and contraptions created to make chores and tasks easier.

They knew nothing of calling a plumber or electrician to fix the toilet or an outlet, instead you would find them rolling up their sleeves or calling over a friend who had a knack for fixing things. Whether it was clothes jammed in the washing tub with the wringer on top pushed against the side of the house, or a leak in the aluminum drum converted to a fish tank for the minnows Big Dad used to go fishing. Before long, it would be back in working condition. I can't tell you how many times we thought the house would blow up when Big Mom got into repairing the gas floor furnace when the pilot wouldn't light. But once someone figured out how to fix something, they would show someone else, sharing their knowledge while being open to suggestions on how to restore it in the future.

Visiting the home they purchased within the city limits was like stepping into a Norman Rockwell country setting. You see, Big Dad owned fourteen hunting dogs, raised chickens in the back yard and had a vegetable garden that produced everything imaginable to feed the entire family a soulful Sunday dinner each day of the week. I'm talking about mustard and collard greens, tomatoes and potatoes, you name it they grew it. I loved the time my cousin, Lynn and I spent on the front porch helping Grandmother shell peas or snap a paper bag full of green beans. Had it not been for the life my grandparents exposed us to while we were young, I would never have known to pick tomatoes while they were still green then place them on the windowsill in the kitchen over the sink so they could ripen over time. In this house, there were lessons to be taught and learned that could not be found in a schoolbook. I'm telling you that my grandparents' home was so "country" that on the weekends we would rake the rocks out of the dirt in the front yard because between the dogs and us kids there was no grass!

This was the house on the block where all of the kids wanted to play. You didn't have to worry about spilling anything on the carpet, because the house didn't have any, just hard wood floors. Don't get me wrong, Big Momma, as everyone in the neighborhood called her, kept a clean house. She and Big Dad just believed that a house "was meant to be lived in". Let me tell you, the best sleeping in the world was on the screened-in front porch during the summer. No mosquitoes got through the screen, and the night sounds sung by the locust and crickets were like a lullaby to put you to sleep.

We never went without food, fun or loving at Big Momma and Big Daddy's house. Every Saturday there was always a group of men playing cards or dominoes under that big oak tree in the front yard, or a game of touch football in the middle of the street. I loved that often times Big Dad would put me on his lap and teach me how to throw down the 'bones' and shout out "fi-deen", when I scored fifteen points. We even had bicycle races up and down the street, after Big Dad and his friends would block it off at the corners so only folk that lived there could get through. It was like a huge block party every weekend, with lots of noise, laughter and pure craziness.

While you could count on Big Mom to give you a good scrubbing in the bathtub, and tight rubber brands around your braids, with Big Dad you could always count on adventure and chaos. He was known for bringing home critters he either caught or found while hunting and fishing. Like the mean possum that he let loose to chase us kids around the back yard until we got tired. Then Big Dad would kill it, clean it and serve it for dinner. He did the same with a big snapping turtle. And although he didn't mind taking me to the creek to go fishing, going hunting was not for girls, according to him. That always made me mad, because I have never been able to get over my fear of guns since I assumed there must have been a reason he wouldn't let me shoot one. Especially since I was such a tomboy and could pretty much do anything the boys in the family could do. His claim that I wouldn't know where to aim it went out the window once my younger brother came back from his hunting trip with Big Dad in tears. Apparently, he couldn't tell the head from the… other end, and shot a rabbit on the side "where the sun don't shine". Robert cried and Big Dad laughed about that for years. And although Robert's mistake wasn't enough to convince Big Dad to take me hunting, I always reminded him that I knew the difference.

A year or so before Big Dad ascended to tickle the funny bone of Jesus, passing away in 1996; he let me witness his wit one last time. While home visiting for the weekend, I decided to hang out with my girlfriend, Kim. Driving through our old stomping ground, we headed to Big Dad's house where we found him sitting out on his front porch smoking his pipe. Inviting us inside out of the heat, he offered us a glass of ice water without the ice, he said, "cause the ice tray in the Frigidaire wasn't frozen yet". It was just about as hot inside, since all he had to circulate the air was an old fan sitting in the middle of the doorway pulling in the hot, stuffy air from the front porch. Kim and I took a seat on the old orange sleeper sofa I had given Big Dad from my college days in the seventies. The multi-colored orange shag rug that covered over half of the musty living room floor didn't appear to have been swept or cleaned since the day I gave it to him, either. As he talked about the last time he went fishing, he put a wad of chewing tobacco under his lower lip, spitting fresh juice in the Folgers can resting next to the sofa.

I learned over the years to pay close attention to everything Big Dad said and did, because you never knew when it might lead to a prank. I have to admit that I thought it a bit peculiar when he made a couple of comments about Kim's painted toenails. It's true she was wearing sandals, but so was I and he didn't comment on my toes. Maybe, I thought, it was because hers were painted fire red.

As we sat in the living room catching up on the happenings since my last visit, I asked how many dogs he had left, since a couple had died and he had given most of them away over the years. Replying he still had four in the back yard, he asked if we wanted to see them, the entire time he never took his eyes off Kim's feet. So after finishing our glass of water, we walked through the dimly lit kitchen and out to the back yard.

Once there, Big Dad asked us to go into the chicken pen to get him a few eggs. Seeing the dogs in the fenced area, the first thing Kim wanted to know was if they would bite. "Oh naw, they won't bother you if you don't bother them", Big Dad replied. That wasn't the most reassuring answer, but we followed him anyway, over to the gate to enter the pen. At this point I couldn't help but wonder why he didn't get the eggs himself, since he was standing right there next to the gate. I really got suspicious when he didn't enter the fenced area of the yard, offering to wait at the gate for us.

Being the daredevil that I am, I went in first followed quite closely by Kim. She was scared but tried not to show it. As we moved closer to the chicken coup, I noticed a big rooster coming toward us. "Big Dad, will that thing bother us?" I wanted to know. "Naw," he said, "it just wants to welcome you into the yard." The rooster came up close behind Kim, but didn't follow us into the chicken coup, so we gathered about a dozen or so eggs then headed back toward the gate. One of the old hound dogs started barking setting off a chain reaction, but they just seemed to be making a lot of noise for the heck of it.

As Kim brought up the rear, I suddenly heard her let out a scream, then another and another. As I hurried toward the gate, I looked back and saw that old rooster pecking at her feet. She tried to run, but it just kept pursuing and pecking. Rushing through the gate, I noticed Big Dad sitting on the steps to the back porch cleaning out his pipe and laughing his head off.

As we fled the back yard, slamming the gate shut, we made it up the stairs through the kitchen not stopping until we reached the front of the house. Kim looked down at her feet, wiping them off and cried, "I'm bleeding". Sure enough, she had small specks of blood coming from her big toe. I could see that there was no serious damage, but I really felt bad. Big Dad followed us back to the living room, chuckling, "I knew that rooster would like those big, plump painted toes of yours." I couldn't believe it; he had set us up, intentionally! He got the biggest kick out of the whole ordeal and said he hadn't had a good laugh in a long time, and then thanked us for coming over.

My Big Dad was quite a character indeed. He liked his RC Cola, Big Red Chewing Tobacco, and above all, he loved to go fishing, hunting and to fix up his old truck. He found humor in the craziest circumstances, and if he couldn't find it, he'd make it. I'd have to say the moral of this story is, don't trust an old man that ain't got nothing better to do than make you a victim of his warped sense of humor. Kim and I are still dear friends, but she never did visit Big Dad with me again after that. Can't say I blame her.

Simply Stated:

Grandparents are a jewel and treasure to have. I can only pray
that future generations will enjoy the longevity most
grandparents of today have with them. We are all living
longer, but not necessarily wiser. We have replaced family
time with the television, work, meetings and computers. The
art of simple letter writing or placing a "how are you doing"
phone call has even been replaced with emails. Although I am
not knocking the advantages of the Internet, I would love to
receive a handwritten letter or to be able to hold one more
conversation with either of my grandparents again. The stories
they shared about their lives should have been recorded, for
they were much more interesting than many of the movies that
have won Oscars over the past decade or the sitcoms on
television today.

What ever happened to family picnics where the teens
taught the "old folk" how to do the latest dances, while being
told it use to be called the jitterbug, or the rock-the-boat, or the
hustle? With all of the advances of technology over the past
twenty-five years, it would be nice to sit and view video tapes
of family reunions with soul train lines, uncles talking smack
and the laughter and tears that make up a family. One of my
few regrets it is that my generation represents the beginning of

our failure to preserve our culture and history. It would be refreshing to have every grandparent living today instill in the younger generations the value of the lessons and stories available to them within their own family and ancestry.

For all of the young adults that lose their way, if you would simply spend some time with a grandparent or a senior citizen in your own family, you will certainly find answers to your life's questions. They are your best hope and resources for the "been there, done that" lessons to be taught. Lessons that will prevent mistakes from being made twice. For, the second time around is not better than the first time when it comes to making a mistake.

Appreciate the little things and the humor of sneaky old grandfathers.

Aj D. Jemison

OAK TREE

"Steal away, steal away, steal away to Jesus"

Ninety-seven years, into my winter the last leaf barely attached
to the branch
Waiting for the breath of Jesus to release me
from my final journey

"Swing down sweet chariot, stop and let me ride"

Had a good life, a long life, a rich life transplanted
with my roots intact
An Arkansas seedling blown to Oklahoma soil

*"Oklahoma, where the wind comes sweeping
down the plain"*

Struggled through the dirt and Midwestern dust bowl
Seeking the nurturing rays of the sun
Never giving up... determined to see the light of day

*"One day at a time, sweet Jesus, that's all
I'm asking of you"*

It was the breath of Jesus that moved that last chunk of dirt,
Opening the life of my oak tree, my ancestors,
To this world

"His eye is on the sparrow, and I know he watches me"

What a sight for these, once virgin eyes first blinded by the
sun's brightness
Struggling to grow, adjusting to the elements
Venturing outside my comfort zone
As I experienced the tornadoes, blistering summers and the ice
storms,
Determined to survive

*"When you walk through a storm,
keep your head up high"*

I found I wasn't alone
Leaves were sprouting, forming my family tree
As I remember, as I reflect, as I rest

"Precious Lord, take my hand, lead me on, let me stand"

Ninety-seven years, don't know why I've held on so long
It was often difficult staying rooted
But the breath of Jesus calmed the storms
What a glorious life for this old oak tree
As the breath of Jesus releases me at last,
The last leaf detaches; my journey is complete...
A history and a path of exposed roots left for others to follow.

*"I will cherish that old rugged cross, and exchange it
someday for a crown"*

Until (Sweet Endings)

"It's so hard to say goodbye to yesterday", so don't. That's what memories are for, to store those yesterdays for when we need them. The person who said that you should forget the past obviously did not have a Grandmother.

I can't remember when she didn't have dusty gray hair, since she told me her first streaks of gray appeared by her 25th birthday. Its texture was course, tough and stringy, perfect for braiding and a pressing comb was a must to create her Sunday "do" for church. The ticking off of seconds on a wristwatch rested on each strand, colored and coated with the past, hers and mine. Hard times, good times, times of joy and times of adversity, all intertwined within the braids she wore from Monday through Saturday.

When you hear the name Big Mama, you probably envision a big bosomed woman with wire-rimmed glasses and a gap between her two front teeth. If so, then your Big Mama must look just like mine. Her spit could heal a cut, slick down an unruly hair and clean a face. And those hands could rub away a broken heart and soothe a sore muscle all in one stroke. Oh yeah, Big Mama was a bible-toting, verse-reciting Christian woman that went to church as much to worship as she did to socialize. Now, I didn't say gossip, because she wouldn't hear of it, and definitely would never admit to it.

My yesterdays with her were a myriad of expressions of love. From the advice she shared on how to cure a sick child to how to be lady-like in words, actions and appearance. She was kindly critical of my work ethic, believing I spent too much time doing for others and not enough for myself. She tried to teach me it is okay to be selfish sometimes, a lesson I still have not mastered. However, I had to remind her that I was faithfully following her lead, for she was the most selfless person I have ever known. Her words were always so comforting; they matched her hands as she could rub my head in such a way to relieve a headache that I never had to take an aspirin. To bring her comfort, I simply had to put on her Mahalia Jackson album and turn up the volume. The gospel melodies would fill the house and lift Grandmother's spirit.

The last time I was home with her before she garnered her wings and boarded her flight to heaven, Grandmother (as I referred to her once I had children of my own, out of respect for her position in the family), had just been released from the hospital. It was a month before the coolness of Christmas showered Oklahoma, coating it with a clean white sheet of snow covered by a layer of sleet. Her feelings about hospitals mirrored all but my mom's, who happened to be a nurse. Grandmother hated the place, the smell, the food and especially those robes that left her chocolate butt hanging in the wind.

My mom wasn't sure if Grandmother would make it out that time, but Grandmother assured me over the phone when I called from Atlanta that by the time I arrived home to visit for Kwanzaa, she would be home as well. As I walked through the front door of her house, there she was sitting in her rocking chair, positioned so she could see everyone's comings and goings. When I asked how she was feeling, she rocked herself forward, slowly stood up, raised her dress to expose her knees (she never wore pants, no true lady should, she would say) and she danced a jig for me right there in the middle of her living room! Her smile spread from her left ear to the right as she sang, "Oh I'm feelin' just fine, 'cause I'm home with Jesus on my mind". Grandmother had a way with words and a song, although she, like my mom, really couldn't hold a tune.

We sat for a couple of hours while she filled me in on the goings on in the family and neighborhood that I'd missed since my last visit. I asked her if there was something special she wanted to do while I was home for the holidays. That gapped grin of hers returned, as she said, "I want to go to the grocery store". I couldn't resist but to ask why the grocery store, so she told me that my mom wouldn't take her, concerned Grandmother didn't possess enough energy to walk the aisles. Grandmother and I kept quite a few secrets between us over the years from the rest of the family, so I told her if she promised not to tell my mom I'd take her. Her cheekbones raised as her eyes beamed. The thrill on her face warmed my spirit, filling me with the same emotion.

Now I don't know if you're familiar with Evangelist Oral Roberts, but my grandmother was a devoted supporter. She mailed him either a $5 bill or five singles the first of every month to help his ministry. "I always get it back," she would say, "sometimes four times more that what I send." I never told her that whenever she gave me the envelope to mail I would open it, take out the cash, add ten or fifteen dollars then sneak it in her panty drawer, or coat pocket or the zipper part of her purse. She had a strong faith, and so did I. My belief was that she would never see that money again if it went to his ministry. Her belief was that the Lord loves a cheerful giver. We both were right.

I decided to add a special excursion to our outing to the grocery store, scheduled for the next day. When I picked her

up, I told her we were going to take a detour first. She loved
surprises so I knew she wouldn't mind. We drove nearly 20
minutes when she realized we were nearing Oral Roberts
University and the City of Faith. She was like a kid at an
amusement park when I informed her we were going to take a
tour through "The Living Bible". It was a 30-minute walking
tour through an automated museum setting of various events in
the Bible. Again, I had to get a promise out of her; that she
would not give me a hard time and would allow me to push her
through the exhibit in a wheelchair. I knew she wasn't going to
swallow this easily, the stubborn woman that she is, but sitting
there in the parking lot leading to the entrance of "The Living
Bible" made it a whole lot easier. She agreed.

The tour was very exciting, with the voice of God
booming as it filled the room of the Creation in surround
sound. Each room told a uniquely animated biblical story with
special affects.   I think I enjoyed it more than she did.
Afterwards, we drove to the neighborhood Safeway store.
Although I wasn't sure if she would still feel up to walking, she
reminded me that she had been riding all day, by car and in the
wheelchair. Grandmother grabbed a shopping cart, explaining
it would give her something to hold on to. Now, I assumed she
had a list and only needed to pick up a few things. What was I

thinking… of course she didn't! Needless to say, we walked every aisle as she kept adding items to the cart.

Reaching the checkout counter, she looks over at me with that gapped grin and says, "I hope you've got some money, because I'm broke". I couldn't believe it, swindled by my own grandmother! I paid for the groceries, loaded them into the car, and home we went. Once parked in her driveway, I circled the car to help her get out of my compact Chevy Manza. Pulling her out of the car was like watching a York Terrier tugging on a St. Bernard, as she began to laugh, causing me to lose my grip. Falling back into the front seat of my car, she said the last thing I expected… "Just wait 'til your momma finds out you took me to the grocery store. She is going to be so mad at you". She laughed so loud and hard she thought, for certain, that she would pee in her pants.

I didn't see the humor in it at the time, but now realize that she really needed just to get out of the house. She had been feeling so helpless and useless since she had taken ill. And for a woman that had cleaned other people's houses, raised their kids and her own, stayed married to the same man for over sixty years and drove a car until her eighty-three year old eyes couldn't see the lines on the road, that was too much to bear. After I helped her into the house and brought in the bags of groceries, we lay across her high bed and took a long nap together. It was a wonderful day.

We brought in the New Year's the same way for over 10 years. The two of us would fall asleep on the floor and sofa watching Dick Clark on television in New York. We would wake up miraculously within minutes before the ball rung in the new year. We would lean over, kiss on the lips, and say "Happy New Year" and "I Love You" then fall right back to sleep. Some four weeks later, my Grandmother took her last ride in the arms of an angel, with wings large enough to hold that big bosomed great-grandmother of seven, grandmother of five and mother of two. She was readmitted into the hospital and the prognosis was looking grim. I remember my last conversation with her over the phone, as I called from Atlanta. I asked if she wanted me to come home. Her reply was transparent to me, because we always had our special code of talking when others were around. She simply said, "I'm ready to go home", and then asked if I knew what she meant.

I asked if my mom was in the room with her. Once she confirmed my mom was sitting there, then I replied, "Yes, Grandmother, I know what you mean, and it is okay". "Are you sure?" she whispered, insinuating that she knew my mom was not ready to let her go. I assured her my mom would be fine, and that she deserved her rest now. I could feel her smile through the phone. We said our last "I love you" followed by the single word "until" then hung up. Grandmother drifted into a coma the next day. A week later, she went "home."

Since her passing, I have envisioned Grandmother back with her brothers and sisters, playing catch up with them and her parents on the life she spent here with us since they left this earth. I find peace in knowing she has completed her cycle of life and returned home to those that shared the beginning of her journey.

Home is a place of comfort and peace. Welcome.

UNTIL, BIG MAMA

Until it is time to join you in glory
Where death is the beginning not end of the story

Until again we meet to laugh, dance and sing
and to know the joy only a home-going can bring

Until that hour of reckoning is upon us one and all
when it's time to rejoice in hearing the Master's call

Until, Big Mama, may our hearts be quiet and still
for it isn't goodbye, for now it is just...
...until.

Life Cycle Two:

LESSONS LEARNED

Wetting the Bed (Manipulation)

For years, I had this reoccurring dream about a baby crying on the floor in a dark room. I always thought it had some meaning or message, you know, like one of those dreams where you are falling, but never hit the bottom. I mentioned it to my grandmother, but she couldn't figure it out either. One day while changing my daughter's pamper, I told my mom about the dream. She gave me the most peculiar look, and asked, "How on earth do you remember back that far?" When I asked what she meant, she sat down on the side of the bed, and began to tell me a story.

I could tell mom was having a vivid memory as she began by telling me that I was that baby. She had this look on her face of sheer disbelief, similar to the one I would have each time my baby daughter would do something that I thought was advanced for a baby her age. Mom told me many nights she and my father would find me in a wet diaper crying on the floor next to my crib. My older brother Vic was almost three years older, so they assumed they knew what to expect from a one-year-old. And since he never fell out of that same crib, they could never figure out how I managed to. She told me the first time they found me on the floor she was sure I had bruises or broken bones. But I had neither, just a wet cloth diaper.

Determined to find out how I landed on the floor, they came up with a plan. Dad repositioned the crib to the center of the room away from the wall, and mom left the door slightly cracked so the light from the living room would shine on the crib without shining in my face while I slept. They took turns keeping watch. Three nights later my mom saw me moving around in the crib. Waking my dad, they both stood next to the door in shock as I slid down the crib railing, sat on the floor and proceeded to wet my diaper. THEN I cried to be changed! She said they couldn't hold back laughing, which only made me cry louder. With their curiosity relieved, mom changed my diaper, and put me back in the crib. Over the next few nights, they saw me play out the same scene night after night. What they witnessed was the fact that I refused to wet the bed.

After hearing this incredible story from my mom, I asked her why she didn't simply put rubber pants on me. She said I hated them, and would cry until she took them off. Even back then, at the tender age one, I made it clear what was and was not "acceptable." I had no desire to lie on wet sheets waiting for someone to eventually change my diaper. Impatient, yes, but somehow I knew that someone would come much sooner if I were sitting on the floor than lying safely in my crib. Over the years, I have slowly learned to be more tolerant, and patient, but I still want what I want when I want it.

Having my diaper changed is one thing, yet causing change was, and still is, a motivator for me. Today, I find that once I identify what I want, I go after it as if it is already mine. And, not surprisingly, eventually it is. It took creativity and skills to slide down that crib railing and not fall or hurt myself. In taking the risk of falling, I ensured that I would not have to tolerate going for a long and uncomfortable period of time in a wet diaper.

Simply Stated:

Too often in life we expect the comfort, but aren't willing to pay the price for it.   Today's generation expect, and unfortunately are provided clothes, entertainment and transportation without a hint of appreciation for the sacrifice parents endure to provide it. And I, regrettably must admit that I am just as guilty, if not more so, than most parents. We have managed to surpass the financial and material wealth of our own parents, yet tend to shower our children with unearned rewards. We have forgotten to teach them how it was acquired, how we perspired coming home everyday tired after trying not to get fired while rising higher up that ladder of so called success.

We enter our homes to a ring around the tub, no toilet paper on the spool, an unmade bed and clothes on the floor. And that's just in our own room! The vacuum hasn't been run, dishes are in the sink and someone over the age of 16 has the nerve to ask, "What for dinner?" It takes work to keep a job, but more importantly, it takes work to raise children. We're obligated to instill in them a sense of responsibility. It is time for us to put their phrase of, "Oh, well" into our own vocabulary. If that nonchalant response works for them, then it surely can work for us to demonstrate that we aren't going to tolerate their behavior any longer.

We might find ourselves less tolerant of the mediocre, and more open to taking a chance, if we are motivated by both our wants and needs. In order to obtain more of what we want, we must now intentionally do things differently, and with conviction. For me, change began with the simple timing of the changing my diapers. I have chosen and adapted to many of the changes that have occurred in my life. Change, my friend, is inevitable.

The pure virtue of patience begins with tolerance for change.

Taking Charge (Responsibility)

I was the built-in babysitter for three of my five siblings. I was the second oldest and the only girl for my first eleven years. Mom always knew she could count on me because I was so "bossy". I made sure everyone did their assigned chores before my mom came home from work as a nursing assistant at Hillcrest Hospital. I was like a drill sergeant! I was so good at giving orders. I took on the responsibility of being in charge because I loved hearing my mom say, "Angel, you are such a help to me." I lived for her praise and approval.

I sought the reassurance of being worthy in her eyes and the eyes of others almost to a fault. For years I have carried internally my apprehension of not measuring up. As a child, fear could easily find its mark within me, especially through critical words spoken by those I loved. I became too good at keeping my pain and fears hidden deep inside. I attempted to camouflage it by the role I took on as mediator to keep the peace, despite my spirit being filled with self-doubt.

I know this world is not perfect. I eventually learned neither is my mom. Her expectations of me were very high at an early age because as she put it, she knew I was very smart. Even though mom had a "reward" system to compensate us, in my opinion it was far from fair. On the meager wages she made working at the hospital, I knew there wasn't much money. That to me really wasn't the issue. I admit I've been known to have an opinion about everything, especially since my favorite phrase is, "my opinion is only worth 2 cents, but I've got a pocket full of pennies." In my opinion, it was never about how much was available. It was more about how it was allocated.

Our weekly allowance was based upon completing our chores, while our "bonus" was based upon the grades we received on our report cards. Recognizing that my brothers had more challenges getting good grades than I did, mom tried to encourage them yet motivate each of us differently. She would reward one of my brothers with fifty cents for a "C", a dollar for a "B" and two dollars for an "A", because school work was really hard for him. Another brother did pretty well in school but was just lazy, so he got fifty cents for a "B" and a dollar for an "A". I, on the other hand, was an honor student, who loved going to school, enjoy competing and was dubbed the "teacher's pet" in most of my classes. Therefore, mom only gave me a quarter for a "B" and fifty cents for each "A"! Now you do the math... this just doesn't seem fair, does it? Her explanation was, "Honey, you get so many "A's" that you still end up with about the same amount of money as your brothers". Basically, she said she would go broke if she had to pay me the same for an "A" as my brother that had to work harder to get one. You tell me, would that motivate YOU to get an "A"?

Naturally, she knew I was far too competitive in school to not make the honor roll just to prove a point to her. But those were hard times for me financially. And needless to say, today I value a dollar a lot less than I value a review of my performance. The lessons mom taught me growing up were not just based upon the importance of education, but also included the importance of responsibility.

When I was seven years old, she sent me to the corner grocery store a few blocks away to pick up some items she needed to prepare dinner. My younger brother, Robert, begged to go with me, and against my wishes, Mom forced me to take him along "to help carry the bags of groceries". The last thing I wanted was my kid brother tagging behind me, especially since he was hardheaded and wouldn't listen. It was a chore to keep him from throwing rocks and jumping off the curb into the street. All I could think about on that walk to the store was that I wanted to wring his little neck. Although it seemed to take forever, it was a very short walk to the store, just three blocks. After going up and down each aisle picking out the items on the list, I walked up to the cash register to pay for the groceries, handing my brother one single bag containing the loaf of bread to carry home.

We left the store and began our trek back home with Robert lagging slowly behind. Halfway there I turned around and noticed that he wasn't carrying anything. He sheepishly said he must have left it on the counter, so back to the store we went. The store clerk insisted the bread wasn't left on the counter and refused to give me another loaf without paying for it again. There wasn't enough money left to buy another one, so we went home without the bread. I was not a happy camper. When I told my mom what happened, she sent me to her room to get the belt from her dresser drawer. Of course, I just knew it was for Robert, as I skipped to the bedroom to get the thickest belt I could find. If I could whistle, I would have done that too. But to my dismay, mom told ME to turn around when I handed her the belt! Asking if she was kidding, she replied that she was going to punish both of us. I was so outdone that I was being punished for him losing the bread that I started crying before the first lick and asked why I was being punished. Her reason- I was the older and responsible one. Even though he got a whipping as well, that was no consolation. In my young opinion, he deserved it, I didn't!

Simply Stated:

As an adult I would have to say that incident in my childhood prepared me for a life of not only being responsible for the actions of others but also, more importantly, dependable to others by my actions. I did not like being held responsible for my brother's lack of it. However, years later I finally understood that my mom trusted my ability to both run the errand and ensure that my brother was accountable for his share. I can now acknowledge that the punishment I received was intended to build my character. Well, Mom, my character is built, strong and fortified. I would just prefer next time that it be built with descriptive words rather than the leather strap of a belt! A simple, "Honey, you should have..." would suffice.

Life's lessons are often unfair and sometimes painful.
But a lesson learned is a lesson remembered.

Unsolicited Help (Taking Control)

Finding amusement in life is surely the anecdote for tough or depressing times. The remedy of laughter and jokes can bring forth the most refreshing tears of joy. Some lessons I've learned have fortunately been sprinkled with humor and occasional laughter.

I'm sure you can remember how your stomach knotted up when a teacher called your mom to come for a meeting after school. Well, try being a young mom getting that first call on your own child. My daughter's kindergarten teacher called me at work on one of "those Mondays"... you know the ones where Murphy's Law was alive and well and in rare form. As I dealt with the craziness of trying to meet Monday deadlines after co-workers called off sick (to recover from their weekend), I received the call from my daughter's teacher requesting my presence in the kindergarten classroom after school. One thing I have learned over the years is never to say, "What now?" or "What else could happen?" I now know it is inevitable that if you mouth those words out loud into the universe, the answer to those questions will not be a welcomed one.

Things weren't looking good as I entered the classroom that afternoon to find my daughter sitting at her desk with her head down. It was clear she had done something she shouldn't have; however, I wasn't nearly prepared for what I was about to find out. As the teacher invited me to sit, I realized that this conversation was going to be as uncomfortable as the tiny chair she was directing me to, as she pointed to one across from her messy desk. All I could think about was how on earth I was going to fit my modest behind in that little chair.

Once seated, she proceeded to share with me the events of the day. Apparently, right before their noon nap, one of her overly energetic students kept leaving his seat to roam the room. The teacher had to ask him repeatedly to return to his seat and finish his work. While she was talking this entire time, my eyes stayed glued to my daughter, wringing her hands and patting her little toes on the tile floor. I couldn't see the connection between this little boy's behavior and my daughter, but I knew there had to be one. The teacher continued, stating that when she left the room for a brief conversation with another teacher in the hallway, she returned to find she had been away longer that she thought, because what she found when she returned was a tale for her memoirs.

She recounted that as she went to sit behind her desk she immediately noticed the roaming little boy crying in his seat. When she asked him to come explain why he was crying, he responded with two simple words, "I can't." Taking this as defiant, she insisted that he get up and come to her desk. The cause of his despair became evident for as he stood, his chair was solidly attached to the seat of his pants! Somewhat in shock, she asked how on earth his chair became stuck to his pants.

He turned, pointed at my daughter and said, "She did it". In total disbelief, she asked Franchiel what she had done. "Well," she began, "he kept getting out of his seat after you told him not to. So I glued him to his chair so he wouldn't get up anymore." Apparently, she had used her entire bottle of Elmer's Glue to make sure he did not get out of his seat again! As you can see, Franchiel felt she had 'helped' the teacher keep her classmate in his seat.

How the teacher managed not to laugh is beyond me because it took every ounce of energy in me not to. Of course, I had the task of explaining to Franchiel why what she did was wrong, inappropriate and not her responsibility. To help make the lesson stick, we took the young boy's chair (and pants) home so that she could clean the glue from them. At first I wasn't sure how to handle this so that a five-year old could understand and take away a lesson. Plus, I had no idea how to remove the glue. After consulting with my mom and grandmother, I just put Franchiel, the chair and the pants in the bathtub, filling it with water and dishwashing liquid. Eventually the glue softened and washed out. It was truly a Kodak moment. As she sat there in that tub of suds and bubbles, I tried to explain to her the reason why she should not have "helped" her teacher. When she quite plainly stated to me, "But mom, I wouldn't have had to help her if she had done it right in the first place," I knew I wasn't getting through. As they say, from the mouth of babes!

At that point, in my life I hadn't experienced enough to know how to explain to my child why what she did wasn't acceptable. So I did what any young mother would do, I asked my grandmother to explain it to her! She kept it simple by asking Franchiel how she would feel if someone moved her favorite teddy bear and she couldn't find it. With a frown, she replied she wouldn't like that at all. Grandmother agreed, adding that the teacher felt the same way when Franchiel tried to discipline the little boy. She should have left him alone and let her teacher handle him. It made sense to my daughter, and taught me how to use examples to explain a lesson.

Simply Stated:

Each one of us at some point in our lives has observed a situation that someone else is trying to handle without success. Even though "helping out" may seem reasonable at the time, we need to realize that by staying out of it and allowing them to handle it, whether they succeed or fail, going through it allows them to grow, also keeping us out of a potentially sticky situation.

Unsolicited help is not always helping at all;
Sometimes you should stick to minding your own business.

Learning By Example (Education)

How many times have you heard someone say, "Repeat after me..." These words are the beginning instructions for memorizing, remembering and learning. When you hear the same words, phrase or sentences over and over, you begin to retain them, planted like a seed in fertile ground.

Back when I was in kindergarten, the classroom walls had large alphabets, numbers and animals on it. I loved being in that room almost as much as my Sunday School class. Learning new things was fun to me. I was like a dry sponge thirsty for water. I was inquisitive, curious and adventuresome. I also loved to share what I learned with other kids in the class that had a hard time getting it. Yes, for me learning came easy.

I recall having finished writing my alphabets one day before the other kids in my kindergarten class. I went into my book bag, pulled out a *Dick and Jane* book and began to "read" it. As my teacher walked by, she stopped behind my chair and saw how I was concentrating on the pages of the book, running my index finger across the pages from the left to the right, line by line. Assuming I was imitating what I had seen someone older do, she jokingly asked what I was "reading". When I responded, "I'm reading about how Dick threw the ball to Jane to keep it from Spot", she looked at me with amazement. Assuming that someone probably had read the book to me, she asked me to read to her, expecting me to talk about the pictures in the book. Instead, I turned back to the first page and actually began to read the story to her, word for word, line by line, page by page. Surprised at my ability to read at 5 years old, she took a closer look and she realized the book I was reading was at the second grade level!

Briefly leaving the room, my teacher returned with the second grade teacher. She had asked her to bring a book from her classroom, again assuming that I might have memorized the story. When I easily read the second book, the second grade teacher asked, "Who taught you to read?"

"My older brother always does his reading and math homework in the TV room at home when I'm trying to watch cartoons," I told them. "My mom helps him with it, but it's hard for him get the words sometimes, so she tells him to 'repeat after me' at least a zillion times." As I continued with my explanation, they just looked at one another in disbelief. "I get mad sometimes because I can't hear my cartoons because they talk so loud and the room is so small. So I go over to see what they are looking at. I try to help my mom teach him the words so they will hurry up and be quiet."

Realizing it was possible for a 5-year-old to read at the second grade level, the teachers created a reading program for the kindergarten class the following year, which has been in existence ever since. See, sometimes it pays to ease drop on someone else's conversation. To this day, one of my favorite things to do is to read anything and everything I can get my hands on. I simply yearn to learn. By the time I got to the fourth grade, some of the teachers requested me to "tutor" my classmates and some younger students. I never thought much of it because I loved reading so much. It just gave me a chance to read more stories.

Simply Stated:

It is said that lifelong learning is the fuel that will ignite the imagination and open the doors to dreams. The match, that lights that flame, can be found by tutoring others. To me, sharing the knowledge you possess with a child or adult is like squeezing the water from a sponge. It opens up room to take in more water. The best part is, you never lose what you've already learned. This is why I encourage school-age children and adults to be a sponge. Take in information, ask questions, and never lose your curiosity. After all, you are not a cat, so it won't kill you. As a matter of fact, it can actual make you more alive than you could ever imagine. Your mind has unlimited storage capacity. Why stop when you can go further. Why wait when you can gain knowledge now. There is no better time than the present, so present yourself with the present of lifelong learning. For wisdom has no age, barriers or restrictions. It is available to us all.

Nothing burns brighter than a turned on mind.

Being a Sponge (Setting Goals)

Being driven is not always a given, especially for a little girl in grade school. I would have to say it was many years later before I realized its meaning. All it took for me to feel that driving force was to see 30 kids on the stage in my elementary school gymnasium one spring day during my third grade year.

Entering the gym at Burroughs Elementary with my homeroom class for an all-school assembly, I noticed right away that one of my older brother's friends was marching up onto the stage with a group of boys and girls. When I asked my homeroom teacher why they were up there, she explained they were participating in the school's Spelling Bee. I was intrigued, watching them nervously staring at all of us sitting on the floor in front of them. I could just imagine how great it must be to be up there on that stage. The thrill of looking out at the entire student body, and waving at their friends, was something I wanted to experience. Once the spelling bee got underway, well, that was all I had to witness to know that I simply had to get up on that stage one day.

After they announced the winner then dismissed us to return to our classrooms, I ran up to my teacher and asked what it would take for me to get up on that stage. "You just have to win the spelling contest in your homeroom," she told me. "Then you can represent your class in the school's Spelling Bee." Well the way I saw it, I had one full year to practice, so practice I did. I had my mom buy me books for older readers, I asked my teacher to give me extra spelling homework, and over the summer months, I read, wrote and spelled words in preparation for the next year's Bee.

They say practice makes perfect, now I know why. When the homeroom contest for the Spelling Bee came around that next year, I was both excited and nervous. Have you ever wanted something so bad that it consumed your every waking hour and spilled over into your dreams? The day of the contest, I was a wreck. My confidence wasn't at its peak, so unfortunately I was the first runner up in my fourth grade homeroom class, not qualifying me to be in the school's Spelling Bee. Disappointed... of course. But devastated, No way! I kept my head up, congratulated the winner and decided that it just wasn't my year to win. I still had next year.

So the cycle began again, as I practiced for another year adding Webster's Dictionary to my reading list. Learning and spelling as many words as I could pronounce, on the day of competition my fifth grade year I was, once again... the first runner up. This left me with two years of not making it to that stage and only one year left before I would be leaving John Burroughs Elementary School to go on to junior high. So, I got strategic. I changed how I practiced and studied to improve my chances. For this last chance of a lifetime, I S-P-E-L-L-E-D E-V-E-R-Y-T-H-I-N-G T-H-A-T I H-A-D T-O S-A-Y. Yes, that's right, I spelled everything that I had to say, and lo' and behold I won my 6th grade homeroom Spelling Bee! Can you imagine going through all of that just to get up on a stage to wave at your friends? But for me it was more than that. I had worked hard, studied hard, prepared myself and it had finally paid off.

On that glorious day of the school Spelling Bee, I marched up the stairs with the other students representing their homeroom classes. My mind was initially on two things: waving at my best girlfriend and keeping my stockings from sagging down my skinny legs to my ankles. As I crossed the stage in front of the entire student body, one of thirty students representing the fourth through sixth grade homerooms, I spotted my girlfriend in the audience. I gave her that "Hey girl, I'm up here" look, with a huge grin. I noticed just behind her was the one girl that didn't like me, who always called me names like the teacher's pet and Miss Smarty-Pants. Of course, I couldn't resist, I had to give her that "Hey girl, I'm up here" look, too, only this time with a smirk!

The contest began as each student took a turn spelling a word. The number of students quickly went from 30, to 25, to 20, to 15, to 10, to five, down to two... this boy and me. And for the first time it dawned on me... I could win this thing! Now remember, all I wanted to do for the past three years was to get up on the stage and wave at my friends. Yet here I was a finalist in my school's Spelling Bee.

My drive kicked in as the two of us spelled one word after another, until after the seventeenth word, he misspelled a word. I got the next one right, I got the next one right, I got the third one right and I won my school Spelling Bee!

Simply Stated:

It pays to have a goal if you never lose sight of it. I never saw my losing in my homeroom during the fourth and fifth grades as a failure; it only made my desire to win that much more intense. I had a simple, singular goal… to get up on that stage. The results of three years of practice was not only meeting but also indeed exceeding my goal. Achievement is possible when one mentally turns impossible into "I'm Possible". It works every time. I'm living proof.

If you believe you can or can't, you're right.

Stand for Something (Leadership)

The more I studied history in school, the more I saw examples of men and women taking responsibility for the actions of others. "We shall overcome" and "By any means necessary" were the buzz phrases of the day when I was growing up. Two points of view with the same end result in mind: equality, fairness and justice for all people. I now understand why and how elected officials, including the Presidents of the United States, are held responsible for the welfare of their hometown constituents and this country's citizens.

You wouldn't think politics would be on the mind of a student such as me, whose least favorite subject was History. Being in junior high school can be quite a traumatic experience within itself without adding the events of the 1960's to it. There were hippies with bell-bottom pants, Black folk with afros, war songs and cries for peace, unity and love. And as a teenager, well think about it; Hormones were raging, experiencing the differences between boys and girls was paramount on a daily basis and peer pressure took over your lives. One of the biggest challenges I had was trying to fit in. I was skinny, wore large framed glasses, had really big eyes and was a book worm. Add to that my extracurricular activities of intramural sports, cheerleading and running for class office. It's a wonder I made it through.

The political bug hit me during this period of my life, as I became increasingly aware of a burning desire to be a leader amongst my peers. The assassinations of two great men, President Kennedy and the Rev. Dr. Martin Luther King, Jr. were the noteworthy events affecting the country back then. One man elected to the highest office in the land to lead a nation, the other born to preach, teach and lead a movement. I always imagined following in their footsteps, so when the opportunity presented itself my ninth grade year, I pursued a political office, so to speak. With a limited number of days to decide what I stood for, followed by weeks of campaigning, I successfully ran for the position of President of the Student Council. In most schools, the student council only affected the selection of after-school activities, the lunch menu or in some cases a limited number of school policies. Winning that election was a milestone for me. But, leave it to me to be in office during a time when I would have to make a major decision that would determine whether or not I would remain Student Council President or be impeached by my classmates.

We lived nearly five miles from Roosevelt Junior High school, and more times than not my brothers and I had to walk to school, since mom had the 7 to 11 shift at the hospital. Checking the weather report each morning was a necessity, to determine what to wear and how the weather conditions would affect our trek to school. We would make up fun games to help take our mind off the distance. Fortunately, on this particular fall morning it was a perfect day for the cloud game. That's where you guess the most characters in the clouds. The sky was filled with a wealth of shapes, sizes and possibilities for the imagination.

With my younger brother Robert in tow, we reached the grounds of Roosevelt Junior High about fifteen minutes before classes were scheduled to begin. However, we were better at guessing the shapes of the clouds that day than what was transpiring in front of our school. It appeared that every Black student, sprinkled with some Whites, was standing on the sidewalk outside the fence that surrounded our school. In the crowd, I noticed some kids carrying handwritten signs that read "Keep Carver Open" and "We Support George Washington Carver Jr. High". The ones with the words "You

Can Bus, Just Not Us" best explained what was going on. You see, there was a decision to be made later that day by the Superintendent of Schools and Board of Education on whether to close Carver Junior High.

As one of a few predominately Black schools on the north side of Tulsa, the decision would determine whether Black students would be bused to several White schools on the south side of town. Segregation meant displacement in our neighborhoods, which was just another form of discrimination since the White students could sleep later and attend their neighborhood schools. Although both junior high schools were rivals in sports, we had a common thread. Most of our parents proudly attended George Washington Carver Junior High and Booker T. Washington High, both Black schools in the neighborhoods where they all lived.

Although Roosevelt's black student body only represented 40% of the school population, we wanted the School Board and media to recognize our support to keep the doors of Carver open. There was one news van parked in the bus drop-off lane in front of the school, with cameras aimed at the students and the signs. As we came upon the gate that led to the school's entrance, several students summoned me over to ask if I was going to cross the picket line. Obviously, I saw this clearly was NOT an option, although in the back of my mind I couldn't help but think about what my mom was going to do to me when she found out I wasn't in class that day. Realizing these students elected me to represent them, I took my place outside the fence and joined in the protest.

When the bell rang announcing the start of first period, all eyes were drawn to the doors of the school, but no one moved. We were nervous, yet here was our opportunity to demonstrate unity. Some five minutes later the Principal's assistant came striding out of the school headed in our, no, in my direction! As she approached, all eyes were fixed on her and what she was about to say or do. She informed me the Principal wanted to see me in his office. Glancing at the students gathering around us, I politely replied, "Could you please ask him to come out here to see me. I can't cross the picket line". Clearly not attempting to hide her displeasure with my response, she indicated the Principal wouldn't be happy with my decision, and then she returned into the school.

Minutes later, she came out again with another message. "It is very important that you follow me to Mr. Turner's office." As respectfully as I could, I repeated my first response, "Could you please ask him to come out here to see me? I can't cross the picket line". It was hard to keep the quiver out of my voice, but I knew what I had to do. The crowd began to cheer and high-five each other as the office assistant once again retreated. Shortly thereafter to all of our surprise, Mr. Turner exited the front doors of the school seemingly headed to confront me personally. He wasn't smiling.

As he came closer, I knew this was going to be the true test of my leadership; simultaneously standing by my peers who elected me to be their leader, while dealing with the principal in a mature manner. All eyes were on me, but mine were totally focused on those of Mr. Turner, with hopes that he could see in mine my need for his understanding and my silent plea for his support. I had never been in trouble and was considered quite levelheaded by both teachers and the administration. I was banking on Mr. Turner remembering that at this very critical moment.

Knowing how important it was that I defuse what might have been construed as a confrontation, as soon as he got within earshot, I began to thank Mr. Turner for coming out to meet with me under the circumstances. In response, he spoke low and even as he asked me to assist him in getting the students to come into the building and go to their classes. With a sense of relief that he was willing to talk it over, I explained the importance of the protest and the need to show solidarity with the students at Carver Jr. High. As he listened to my voice of reason, he actually said he understood!

He asked me to walk with him while he explained that for the safety of the students we would have to either enter the school building or leave the property and return home. Understanding his position and request, being the negotiator that I am, I told him I did have one small "demand" (of course, it was a request, but I had to perpetrate as if I had some clout.) I asked if all students participating in the protest could get an excused absence for the day if they chose to go home. He actually agreed, which resulted in more high-fives and cheers. I did it! I couldn't believe I managed to both represent and serve my peers without upsetting the administration. Not bad for a ninth grader, wouldn't you say?

Now several police parked cars along the sidewalk just in case there was a problem. I asked Mr. Turner to talk to them for us, promising that the students would remain peaceful. He requested the officer in charge to instruct his officers to follow at a reasonable distance behind the students that chose to return home. Once they agree, I called the students together and explained their choices, to either go to class or leave the school property and return home. Of course, many wanted to stay and continue the protest, but the media had already come and gone, so I encouraged them to go home since the cameras would not be returning and we were already guaranteed to be on the 5 o'clock news. Some rebel-rousers were reluctant but were eventually persuaded by the rest of us. So we began the long walk home. The moment I got in the house I called my mom to explain what happened and that Robert and I were both safe at home. Fortunate for me, my mom was okay with my decision to represent my classmates, adding that she was proud of me.

Simply Stated:

Standing up for what is right and the rights of others is so very important. And when you can have a victory at the end of the day, well that makes it all worth it. Not only has George Washington Carver Junior High remained open, but today it is a magnet school attracting many white students from the south side. Not bad, not bad at all! I know we can't take a lot of the credit, but we did our small part. It takes so little to make a difference, like a single drop of rain from the sky can eventually make its way to a raging river or the ocean.

Just think, from the time I began to write this book to this day as it is about to go to press, our country is at war again. I can only pray that those in positions of leadership and power will realize their clout and ability to serve us, the voters that put them into office. And if you didn't vote, shame on you for not being a **Voice Of The Election** (VOTE) that put them there (or kept others out). I hope that our nation's leaders will protect us, in addition to our loved ones and young ones both male and female; we have been deployed to fight this war for the liberation of others in a state of oppression. They are all trying to do their small part to make a big difference in the lives of those overseas and right here in the USA. We are depending on the ability of our political leaders and military to make the right decisions and to bring our troops home safely. And hopefully when this war is over, we will turn our attention and focus on fighting the war of poverty, illiteracy, homelessness and helplessness right here in the United States of America.

Stand for something or you'll fall for anything.

"INSPIRATION"

With you as my inspiration
I continue to soar,
my feet off the earth,
floating higher and higher
beyond my wildest dreams...

And though the winds may
seem to be the source of the
heights I achieve,
I know that it is actually you.

And then to look to my right
and see you there soaring
beside me,
I am inspired to continue
onward and upward.

I am so happy to have you in
my life, and look forward to the
tomorrows we will create.

Life Cycle Three:

DEFINING MOMENTS

Aj D. Jemison

JAZZ

Fluid movement with tantalizing strokes

A building desire fills the air

Clashing waves rising and falling

A caressing rescinding tide follows,

This is the ecstacy of JAZZ...!

Raising the Phoenix (Thankful)

It was a Friday, not the 13th but it sure felt like it. The air was filled with that uneasy feeling you get early in the day that something is going to happen, something you can't quite put your finger on, you just feel it.

This May morning began that way, but as the day progressed, I chalked it up to letting my imagination run wild. I got home from work about 7pm, which is early for me, especially being in the retail business. Ascending one flight of stairs to my second floor flat, I dropped my keys in the place I could always find them, on the floor next to the front door. I could hear my daughter was already home chatting away on the telephone. Fixing a bite to eat, I stripped down to a t-shirt and pair of sweat pants, then laid out on the couch to surf the cable channels. It must have been close to 10pm when this eerie feeling woke me to a dark apartment, except for the glow of light coming through the open patio door. As I lay there, I notice a flickering orange-tint to the light shining through the glass. At first I thought it was the college students I saw earlier when I arrived home, moving out of their unit downstairs. They were loading a moving truck earlier, so I assumed they were backing it up onto the grass to load some heavy furniture.

But there was something odd about the light. I could hear my daughter in her bedroom still talking on the phone. I asked her who she was talking to for so long. She replied her grandmother and Aunt Vicki in Oklahoma. Through laughter, she never missed a beat, resuming her conversation with them. The aura of light was intensifying, getting the best of my curiosity. I rolled off the couch and walked casually over to the patio. Living in an upstairs unit had its advantages, because I could see the entire courtyard and pool area on the rear side of the complex's management office.

As I opened the patio door, I notice there was no breeze. It was relatively quiet, with no sign of my neighboring students or a moving truck. The direction of the light seemed to be coming from overhead, behind me, but it just didn't make sense. Its blazing brightness illuminated both the sky and the trees. I closed the door but couldn't shake the feeling, so I walked over to my front door to look out on the landing. First glancing to the left down the stair, I found it empty of people and sound. But as I turned to look to my right a panic overtook and shook me to my bones. A wall of fire was consuming the ceiling at the rear of the building, etching its way toward the unit next door to mine.

I switched out of my panic mode into automatic survival, my first thought to protect my daughter. I ran back inside screaming to her to get out of the house. She entered the living room with a stunned look, unable to react as I grabbed and pushed her out of the front door, down the stairs. She still had the cordless phone in her hand and began to yell to my mom over the phone that our building was on fire.

Trying to think what to do next, I ran back into the house, slipped my feet into shoes lying next to the couch grabbed my purse and Franklin Planner then hurried back into the hallway. Forgetting to pick up my keys off the floor, I remember consciously leaving the front door open and unlock, figuring that it would make access easier for the firemen, hopeful they would do less damage to my apartment this way. By now, I could feel the heat from the flames, hear the cracking of dry wood burning and smell the pungent odor of black smoke. As my daughter yelled to me to join her from the yard in front of the building, I took one more turn toward the fire to knock on the doors of my three upstairs neighbors to make certain they were out. Hearing no response, I stumbled down the stairs. With a final thought of the elderly gentleman that lived below me, I turned once more to pound on his door to ensure he had made it out safely as well. Again hearing no response, I sprinted toward the front door as the bellowing smoke began to consume the hallway.

By this time, I could hear the sirens of the fire trucks approaching from a distance. As I exited the building to find people gathering in the courtyard, Franchiel ran sobbing into my arms, still holding the cordless phone. I could hear my mom screaming questions from the receiver, but couldn't answer her as I held and consoled my daughter. Seeing the fire engine gave a false sense of relief that our unit might only sustain smoke and water damage, since it was located in the front of the building, further away from the fire. But time passed slowly as Murphy's Law took hold. First, the firefighters couldn't find a working water hydrant, and then they couldn't get the hose close enough in time to save the building.

I always thought that it was special effects when I'd see a rolling fireball in a burning scene on television. But that cool May night in the suburbs of Detroit I witnessed the actual rolling of a fireball from where I stood in that courtyard through my open patio window. I saw it enter my open front door like an intruder, engulfing the couch I had been napping on less than a half hour earlier. It gracefully swept through the kitchen then on into the bedrooms, out of sight. I knew the actual moment it entered my daughter's room because that was when the phone line went dead on the cordless phone that she was gripping. As I held my sobbing 21-year old daughter, caressing her hair, I just kept repeating the words, "Thank you, Jesus. Thank you, Jesus." Her tear-stained face looked up at me with eyes filled with fear and anger, asking, "What are you thanking him for? We lost everything!" My response was so calm, so reassuring and so true. Taking a deep breath then exhaling, I replied, "We didn't lose everything, baby. I have you in my arms. You and I are standing here holding each other. I am thanking Him for that."

With those words, I knew everything would be all right. For despite the material losses in the fire that night, we had salvaged the most important thing... our faith. The following day I went to my office at the mall to make necessary calls and take care of other personal matters. The news of my misfortune spread like that fireball, as many mall and store employees stopped by to express their concern and offer personal and financial assistance. Not accustomed to receiving help it was quite difficult to keep my tears in check, but I managed to do just that as I reassured all of them that we would be just fine. But it was the visit from Anita, a department store manager, that reminded me that I was right to remain faithful.

Hearing that I was in the office, she stopped by to give me two pieces of news. I remember telling her to "give me the bad news first, because I'm on a roll", still holding onto my sense of humor. Anita told me she was moving back to New York in a week to manage a store, closer to her hometown. I congratulated her, expressing how much I appreciated her friendship. She then told me the "good news", which was filled with blessings. Her company was relocating her so she would be residing in an executive suite for up to three months. In the meantime, the rent on her high-rise apartment downtown overlooking the Detroit River was paid through August. She offered it to me, along with the use of her furniture, until she found a permanent place by early fall. I not only would have a place to live, but it was furnished and rent-free through the summer. God is good, all the time!

From the ashes that once were our earthly belongings, rose the phoenix of faith to guide us upward. The only thing that brought me to tears about the fire was the loss of pictures of my children and family. But with a non-wavering faith, they, too, were replaced from an unexpected angel. On my 40th birthday that July 15th, I received a small box from my former husband, with whom I share the same birth date. Three years earlier, I had mailed him one of those "Over Forty" Birthday cards. When I opened the card attached to the box was the same card I had sent him on his 40th birthday with a note that he had held onto that card for three years just to send it back to me. Then I opened the box and couldn't contain my tears. Not only had he sent me a box full of pictures of our kids, it also contained pictures of my family that he found in his belongings after our divorce. It was the best birthday present I ever could have received.

Simply Stated:

It is one thing to say that you have faith and believe in the Lord. It is how you manifest your faith that unblocks the blessings you are meant to receive. Your faith will be tested many times, but if you learn to give thanks everyday for what you have, you will pass the test and receive another blessing as a reward.

Ye of so little faith, wait on the Lord. Wait, I say, on the Lord.

MY WARM SEPTEMBER

Remembering... reflections of worthwhile memories
Wishes, hopes, thoughts that once were today
Now forever trapped in my mind and my heart
Like my warm September...
thoughts of me with you

Touch my heart; yes, you did, leaving an indelible imprint
Your smell a fleeting scent that I can't forget
The freshness of your smile and laughter
Sharing my warm September...
My days with you, far too short.

It's cool now as I seek warmth from within
Another fall breeze chilling my soul and peace
The clouds move swiftly, passing with each tick-tock
My warm September...
Remembering, reflecting, releasing you.

"I too have a dream"

Aj D. Jemison

Wake Up (Challenges)

In the spirit of Dr. Martin Luther King, Jr., we come together each January as a reminder to remember, celebrate and renew the dream of a man, a visionary, and a dreamer. It is said that the true dreamer plants seeds for the next generation. At some point, many of us have dreamed of making a difference in the life of a young person. The truth found within each of us is a teacher of life's lessons. In celebration of Dr. King's holiday each year, many acknowledge that our children are the future of this country. As parents and adults, we pray that they will possess a dream to grow into contributing, responsible adults. And for those who support these dreamers, we do so because we recognize they will need our encouragement to make it through the rough times.

Recognizing the importance of education, whether on the giving or receiving end, it is critical that we maximum its capacity through our efforts. So my question to you is, "Are you just awakening from a short nap, or have you slumbered too long?" It has become clear to me that only by being fully rested can we be fully prepared. A full night's sleep filled with visions and dreams, will provide a full recharging of our energy. Only then can we be engaged with the necessary tools to truly make a difference.

No one is perfect, and I am no exception. I made many decisions that could have negatively affected the rest of my life. Married at 18, a mother at 19, I took the rockier road with it curves and steep hills rather than following the standard road map to success. Stopping short of my destination and giving up, however, were NOT options! I gave birth to my first-born five days before taking final exams at the end of my freshman year in college (passing with three A's and two B's). Nearly seven years later, I walked across a stage seven months pregnant, to receive a two-year Associates Degree. Despite taking seven years to achieve a two-year degree, one of my proudest accomplishments has been managing to raise two children after two divorces without governmental assistance.

At the age of twenty-five, I dreamed of one day managing a million square foot shopping mall by my 40th birthday. I realized that dream by my 34th birthday, then was promoted to manage a 1,500,000 square foot mall 18 months later. Three years ago I was charged with overseeing and opening a brand new mall in Florida. Yes, I have been most blessed and am forever thankful for the dreams I have fulfilled so far in my lifetime. And I am pleased to say that "I ain't done yet!"

The challenges that come with taking the road less traveled are many. Being viewed as different, or not focused, or living in a dream world are labels often times bestowed on such a creative being. But it has been my charge and responsibility to nurture and encourage those creative juices that flow through the veins of my children. A strong push and many pulls go along with raising a child that sees the world through psychedelic lenses. Having confidence that their day of triumph is right around the corner is what will be most remembered when a child breaks through and explodes on the scene with the unexpected. That tomorrow is in the near not distant future, of that I am certain.

When I moved to Atlanta in 1986, I had the privilege of working for the Martin Luther King Center for Nonviolent Social Change. There I worked on the celebration for the Second Anniversary of the National MLK Holiday and became familiar with Dr. King's writings, speeches and sermons. His words and actions shook a nation awake before his untimely death. Today we are obligated to be teachers by example, demonstrating to our youth and communities how to "do" something and not simply give lip service.

Aj D. Jemison

In the early 60's there was a commitment and determination that brought about the right to vote, the enforcement of open housing and the eventual hiring of minorities and promotion of women across this nation. Yet, with all of these accomplishments in the 60s, and 70s, we have entered the new millennium with a sense of helplessness. On September 11, 2001 the dream turned into a nightmare, shaking our nation awake to a terrorism we never dreamed would hit right here in our home, the United States of America. We came together as a nation, wearing the colors of our flag, with all of the adjectives removed. We were no longer African-American, Native-American, Latino-American or Asian American... we were simply AMERICAN!

Do you realize that of all of the holidays celebrated by the citizens of these United States, **this** holiday was created not to honor a man but to honor his dream for our country? Dr. King lit a fire under the feet of a nation. We now have a responsibility to rekindle that flame. We've always had a reason, now is the season to get motivated so that the message becomes clear...the importance of having a dream and striving to live it.

Hanging on the wall in my office is a large painting entitled *He Ain't Heavy* by artist Gilbert Young. It depicts a person leaning over a wall, reaching down to lend a helping hand to another. I had the privilege of meeting Mr. Young at the African Arts Festival in downtown Detroit several years ago. I explained to him how this particular piece of his work moved me to reference it in most of my speaking engagement at schools and universities across the country. Expressing that although it may look as though the main point of the painting is the need to help someone less fortunate, it is what I visualize BEYOND the picture frame which motivates me. I told him, "Beyond the frame is a higher, steeper wall, and had it not been for that person (a reflection of me) reaching back to help up another, I wouldn't have his shoulders to stand on to get over the next, higher wall." I added, "the sky you have painted, Mr. Young, reflects the limits to anything I want to accomplish."

Years ago Dr. King was beaten down but stood his ground, never faltering in faith and purpose. In the words of gospel singer, Donnie McClurkin, "a saint is just a sinner who fell down and got up. We all fall down, but we can get back up again." As a people and a nation we have fallen down over the years, exchanging caring with complacency in so many arenas.

We have fallen down in our school systems, but we can get back up again by mentoring a child, encouraging higher wages for our teachers, and going back to school as adults to hone our skills to be better prepared for the future.

We have fallen down in health care, but we can get back up again by providing funding for the research to cure diseases such as Sickle Cell Anemia, Lung, Breast and Prostate Cancer. We also can get up by holding our nursing homes accountable for the treatment and care our elderly, remembering they are OUR parents and grandparents.

We have fallen down in providing available jobs for the jobless, but can get back up again by supporting the local Chambers of Commerce and Urban Leagues to attract and encourage more businesses and industries to relocate and build in our hometowns.

And even though our spirits fell down with the twin towers of the World Trade Center and the plane crashes on Sept 11th, BEFORE we get back up again we should be rolling over onto our knees to pray for our families, for our country, for mankind. We should be lining up in front of churches across this country on Sunday mornings like we do at football stadiums on Sunday afternoons. We should send encouragement to our military, many mere teens, young adults and women, for their efforts to help us all regain a sense of security again on this American soil.

Yes, Dr. King had a dream and he gave us hope. When he led the song, "We Shall Overcome", it was a prophecy, a prediction, and a promise. I, personally, not only believed in his dream as a little girl of the 60s, I believe in it today as a mother of the new millennium. I, too have a dream, today. I challenge you to dream. The clock is ticking.... It's time, and I dare you, to wake up.

I can do all things through Christ who strengthens me.

Where Is Your Vision

Where *is your vision, your vision for thousands...*
...who are unable, unaware or just unwilling to believe in the possibility that you are capable and can improve your way of living

How *is your vision, your vision for thousands...*
...going to change thinking into doing what must be done, to teach that we can get along, to run on and on until the victory is won

What *is your vision, your vision for thousands...*
... will it aid in your dedication to the creation of improved education for our young, developing their growth, their minds and their visions?

When *is your vision, your vision for thousands...*
...going to see beyond the line of color, the lines of politics, the lines of unemployment and the line of fire to lead our communities into a productive, progressive and promising future

Who *are the visions, the visions for thousands...*
... those willing to make a difference by taking the time, to take a stand in taking the lead toward a brighter future, a healthier community, and a united people

We are the vision, the vision of thousands...
...we are the lives lost and those found, we are those who fought to regain control over terrorism, even knowing it might, it would, it did cost so many lives;

...we are the tears shed, the mouths fed, the voices heard with each meaningful word;
...we are the talent required, the unemployed hired, the phoenix from the fire with a strength in our desire to not take it lying down and not be pushed around;

...we are the reason there will be a brighter tomorrow after so much sorrow, the driver behind the wheel as we continue to appeal to our nation, our world, to simple care for one another like a sister or a brother.

Oh, what a vision, this vision for thousands...Our vision is clear...
We are the present **and** the future.

Carpe Diem!!!

I Dare You (Consequences)

It's funny how the words "I dare you" can quickly bring us to action, even if we know the likelihood of getting in trouble are pretty high. But we take that dare and we take our chances. My brothers' friends were always daring me when we were young. My brothers would warn them, "I wouldn't dare Aj, if I were you". But their poor friends just wouldn't listen or didn't know any better. And the last thing you wanted to do was to dare me to do something "to" you. Without a doubt, you would end up on the losing end of the dare.

Unfortunately for my older brother on one occasion he didn't follow his own advice. There was the time when we were teenagers that Vic kept bothering me when I was working on a project in the middle of the floor of his bedroom. He just wouldn't leave me alone, teasing me and pulling on my hair. So when I'd had enough, I reminded him that he would regret it if he didn't stop. Needless to say, he didn't heed my warning. I knew he would mess with me again, so as I quickly scanned the room and out of the corner of my eye spotted my payback… a big, orange purse lying on the floor near the closet door. When Vic went to touch me again, in a split second I lunged for the purse and with all my might threw it at him. Just as quickly, he ducked just in time for the purse to go sailing past his forehead, missing it by inches, striking the top window pane over his bed. The glass shattered, making a loud crashing sound.

Mom came rushing into the bedroom from the kitchen glaring at us both when she saw the broken glass. "Who did that?" she yelled. Simultaneously pointing at each other we shouted, "He/She did it!" Mom was not amused. Vic figured if he spoke first she'd believe him, so pointing at the floor he rapidly explained, "She threw that purse at me and broke the window". My immediate explanation to prove it was his fault was, "Yeah, but HE ducked!"

Years later after Vic left home for college, Mom converted his bedroom into a den. But that section of the window pane is still broken today, some thirty years later. Mom never replaced it saying it would serve as our reminder of how a simply annoyance can result in damage that may never be repaired or replaced. Memories of the orange purse have come to mind many times over the years when I have encountered making tough decisions and considering the consequences.

Facing challenges is a part of life; some minor ones some major ones, all requiring a difficult decision. The outcomes are the reminders and lessons we learn. History is filled with stories, lessons and reminders that direct us to take action, preferably positive ones that will result in fewer broken windows, broken promises or broken hearts that cannot be mended.

MY PURPOSE

I stand looking into the family photos on the shelf
Gazing into the eyes of my ancestors seeking the answers
To my purpose
Big and brown, into the windows to their souls I stare
Praying for direction, guidance a simple sign to guide me
To my purpose

My eyes are those of my father, beautiful and inviting
Yet filled with such sorrow and pain hiding the path and journey
To my purpose
My lover's heart remains just beyond reach of my own
While I sit alone in my bedroom wishing him to be the destiny
To my purpose

The eyes of my children will never know the tears shed
Out of fear that they will never know they're the resulting arrows
To my purpose
And finally it all comes together and I have answers
My God has opened my eyes to his detailed roadmap
To my purpose

I have been on this journey, sharing, caring, loving and daring
My purpose, simply to have you read this and think, while you
Consider your purpose.
My purpose was always simple… to matter to someone
To care for and love someone, to give of myself to the fullest,
My purpose has been fulfilled.

Acknowledgements

"While on others thou art calling, do not pass me by."

My first "thank you" is always to my Lord and Savior for His wisdom and compassion. He planted my seed in the womb of Gladys Mae Henderson Turner. Through you, Mom, God has blessed me with a precious nurturer, teacher and breath of fresh air to ensure there is always a breeze beneath my wings.

I brag with pride about being the Little AJ to the Big AJ, my "Dad", Arthur Lee Jefferson. Dad, you have been my reliable advisor, thoughtful and clear. You are a rare good man and I am forever thankful for the joy and peace you bring to our family. Your gentle spirit will forever whisper prayers of love in my heart.

To my daughter, K. Franchiel, your light is only dimmed by the covers you pull over your head in fear of revealing how big your heart truly is. You grew from a pouting little girl to a statuesque young woman with unfulfilled dreams grander than your life could realize. Your clock is still ticking and the alarm will soon ring to announce that you have arrived to that destiny you have so painstakingly sought.

To my son, Houston, I thank you babe for having the same response of "Always" when I tell you to be careful. It is so reassuring, and I know that you will be protected "always" by the brown angels that embrace you with their massive wings. I applaud your desire to follow your heart and step out on faith to pursue your dreams as you seek your place in life and on this planet.

This project could never have occurred without the "pushers" in my life. Ricc Rollins, you shoved me out of my comfort zone to write this book, and for that I am thankful. You are one of the few people that could tell me "no" on one of those rare occasions when I wanted to throw in the towel. And thanks to you, Lorenzo Robertson, for your gentle spirit was always there to encourage me.

I am also grateful to the other female AJs in my life. Angela Judge your enhancements and understanding of the English language makes me sound good, and to my girl AJ the DJ you provided my stress reliever with the many jazz CDs you send from Detroit which kept me focused, mellow and inspired (especially Will Downing)!

To my siblings, Vic, Robert, Dail, Vincent and Tori, with whom I have passed through this life and shared many adventures and memories, I am so thankful. To Vic for being my rock; Robert for transforming one of my first poems into a song when we were kids and entrusting me with your little lady; Dail for demonstrating unconditional love; Vincent for the phone calls at just the right time; and to my sister, Tori, what can I say, girl? You have Grandmother's (Big Momma's) caring spirit when it comes to taking care of sick kids and family members. Thank you all, my brothers and sister for (lovingly) giving me a hard time and forgiving me when I returned it in spades.

To Gwen and Jennifer Turner, thanks for providing love to my brothers. To Gregory Richard Jemison, as much as I hated the pedestal you put me on years ago, I am grateful that you thought I belonged up there. Brenda, thanks for being Houston's "other mother" and for sharing in the good and tough times with my (our) kids.

To my nieces and nephews, the pebbles in my life that are the future divas and producers of tomorrow: Ciara and Michaiah Wilson, and the Turner clan: Robin, Shawntavia, Dawnjulae, Jessica, Vincent, Katia, Victoria and Naya Turner. I know each of you will stomp your mark on this earth because you all come from the best stock.

To my "fresh air", Tom, I can't thank you enough for forcing open the windows to my true self. Because of you I can now not only think outside the box, but I can experience the joys of life that reside there. Having the wind in my face on a Gold Wing is an exhilarating feeling. And now riding on my own *Suga-Baby* is the highlight of my second wind. Thanks for exposing me to riding and allowing me to share it with you.

To the Buffalo Soldiers Motorcycle Club I give thanks for a family of bikers that have encouraged my adventurous self. You are one of the most caring group of people I have had the privilege to proudly travel this country. It is my honor to be "Suga Soldier". Ready and Forward, my brothers and sisters.

To Felicia Wintons, your love for the word and books has resulted in many bound pages that encourage thought. Thanks for allowing me to put pages in your hands and your Tampa store, Books for Thought.

Special thanks to my many "sistas" for being there for me and the teachers that kept me grounded when needed, yet allowed me to soar when necessary. Linda Ball, Jean Derrico, Kim Midget-Jones, Diane Hughes Pollard, Suelen Smith, Mrs. Gilliam, Mrs. Chapman, Rita Kitts Brandin, Barbara Shannon Banister, Glenda Roberts Evans, Velma Sims, Joyce Clark, Cletta Rowden, Wilma Terrell, Ava Demonja, Delores Lang,

Millicent Compton, Granny Harris, Julia Belcher, Sonja Maccagnone, Congresswoman Carolyn Cheeks Kilpatrick, Sheila Simmons, Bonita Elias, Carolyn Lighty, Yolanda Anthony, Pat Dawson, Donna Russell Crum, Susan Casper, Joy Petit, Secily Wilson, Connie "Cottoncandi" Holloway, Pat "Black Ivory" Wright, Amelia "Lil Dog" Thompson, Lynne "Red" Crowley, Simone "Journey" Gamble, Denise "Baby Cakes" Leverett and Nina "Dark Diva" Dawson. Ladies, you all have been my role models for class, wit, spunk, heart and integrity.

To the loves of my life, thanks for sharing yours with me.

To my many adopted children across the United States: Brittanie, Nikki, Big Keisha, Little Kisha, Tyronda, Janita, Ben, Tisa, Bryanna, Shereka and Latasha...STAY FOCUSED.

Finally, I thank my extended family and friends from Arkansas, Oklahoma, Georgia, Colorado, Michigan and Florida. I hope what I returned to you was enough. Most of you are still walking on this side of the clouds, while the spirit of others frees them to read this over my shoulder. Because you have taken me under your wings for protection during the storms I have encountered, I can now take flight and use my wings to protect and guide others. You have taught me well, and now this student has become the teacher.

So, from Angela Turner, "Angel", Angie Outley and Aj D. Jemison, I say, THANKS... *from this brown angel to another.*

About the Author

Recognized as a community leader in the many cities she has called home, Aj D. Jemison has been a trailblazer as one of the first African American women to manage a shopping mall. She has been honored as One of the 100 Most Distinguished African American Women of Detroit, and recently as the Tampa Bay Minority Businessperson of the Year. Her "up close and personal" approach of introducing the opportunities that exist in the retail industry to women and school age children, has ignited thousands to pursue and achieve their dreams.

Aj has committed thousands of hours volunteering to promote education, the adoption of minority children, the encouragement of teens and the advancement of women in the workplace. Aj is currently working on her first children's book and a book of poetry. She resides in Tampa, Florida. You can visit her website: www.JustAj.com.

If you would like to order additional
copies of

Just Aj! simply stated

please photocopy the order form
and mail it along with your
check, money order
or credit card payment to:

JustAj! Communications, LLC
4532 West Kennedy Boulevard
Suite #435
Tampa, Florida 33609

(please print)

Name: _____

Address: _____

Address 2: _____

City, State: _____ Zip;_____

Phone: (_____) _____

E-Mail: _____

I would like to order _____ copies of JustAj! simply stated @ $15.00 each+$4.95 (s/h)
(add $1.00 for shipping per additional copy)

Please autograph the book for_____

[   ] Check   [   ] Money Order   [   ] VISA , MC, AMEX (please circle one)

Name of Cardholder: _____

CC# _____ 3- DigitSecurity Code _____

Expiration Date: _____/_____ (MM/YY)

Signature: X_____